Thérèse of Lisieux
A Biography

Patricia O'Connor

Our Sunday Visitor Publishing Division
Our Sunday Visitor, Inc.
Huntington, Indiana 46750

Permission has been granted to the author to reprint excerpts from the following books:

Story of a Soul, translated by John Clarke, O.C.D. Copyright © 1975, 1976 by Washington Province of Discalced Carmelites ICS Publications, 2131 Lincoln Road, N.E., Washington, D.C. 20002

St. Thérèse of Lisieux: Her Last Conversations, translated by John Clarke, O.C.D. Copyright © 1977 by Washington Provinceof Discalced Carmelites ICS Publications, 2131 Lincoln Road, N.E., Washington, D.C. 20002

St. Thérèse of Lisieux General Correspondence I, translated by John Clarke, O.C.D. Copyright © 1982 by Washington Province of Discalced Carmelites ICS Publications, 2131 Lincoln Road, N.E., Washington, D.C. 20002

Photographs are provided through the courtesy of Office Central de Lisieux, Lisieux, France.

Copyright © 1983 by Our Sunday Visitor, Inc.
200 Noll Plaza, Huntington, Indiana 46750

All rights reserved. No part of this book may be used or reproduced in any manner whatsoever without written permission except in the case of brief quotations embodied in critical articles and reviews.

Library of Congress Catalogue No: 83-63169
ISBN 0-87973-607-0

Printed in the United States of America

For
Josephine Moore
and
Edward J. O'Connor

Acknowledgements

To disentangle the details of Thérèse Martin's real life from the legend of the Little Flower has taken many scholars years of work. Only because of their meticulous review of hundreds of pages of sources is it now possible to write a concrete account of her life. I am indebted to:

Father André Combes, the first scholar to work with Thérèse's original writings and the man who persuaded the Martin sisters to agree to an "exact and complete" edition of Thérèse's letters. Everything published before Father Combes' arrival at the Carmel in 1946 had been doctored.

Father François de Sainte Marie, O.C.D., who prepared the texts for a facsimile edition of the original manuscripts that comprised Thérèse's autobiography. These Father François de Sainte Marie had published in 1957 as the *manuscrits autobiographiques*.

The research team that spent eight years reviewing all the conversations recorded by Thérèse's sisters and others during the last few months of her life, as well as all medical records of her illness, to produce the detailed and accurate *Derniers Entretiens*, published in 1971.

Father John Clarke, O.C.D., who translated into English the first volume of the *General Correspondence*, the authenticated version of *The Story of a Soul*, and shortened version of *Derniers Entretiens*. It is to Father Clarke and the Institute of Carmelite Studies that I owe my most immediate debt for allowing me to use his precise and beautiful translations.

I also want to thank Albert Larose and his staff at the Thomas Library, Wittenberg University, for locating and obtaining the necessary French sources, and Rosemarie Burley for typing the manuscript.

Finally, I am especially grateful to the American Philosophical Society for a research grant enabling me to visit Lisieux; Leanne Wierenga and Michèle Boisseau for their help with translation; and the prioress and community of the Carmel of Lisieux for opening their archives to me and for graciously answering so many questions.

Patricia O'Connor

Contents

INTRODUCTION

She wasn't exactly pretty; her chin was a little large, but she had marvelous blonde hair and a touching air of innocence.

Mother St. Léon and Mother Stanislaus
Teachers at the Benedictine Abbey, Lisieux[1]

When people began to whisper the word "saint" along with her name, Thérèse (teh-réz) Martin passed out of the world of a real human being with a slightly large chin into clouds of sentiment. She became "angelic," and took on "a heavenly expression." Even though she lived in our age of photography, she was shown to the world through a haloed, heavily tinted portrait. The very name Thérèse of Lisieux evokes a sense of the remote — ancient or medieval times when people were known by their towns. Like any French girl born in the 1870s, she had a last name. Her father, Louis Martin, lost 50,000 francs on the Panama Canal[2] and Thérèse had a pet dog named Tom. Thérèse Martin became a victim of the impulse to edify, a victim of other people's notions of the saintly.

By the time she was born in 1873, the Romantic Era was a little tarnished. Six editions of Darwin's *Origin of Species* had sold out in 13 years, heralding a new way of looking at old, fixed truths. Thérèse had an observant, honest mind. Of a pilgrimage to Rome at age 14, she said, "I always had to find a way of *touching everything*."[3] Like all girls trained in the convent schools of the 1880s, she was taught proper penmanship — graceful, slanted, artifi-

1

cial. In Thérèse's case, the lesson didn't take. She later shifted back to the script that was natural to her — straight up and down.[4]

Her town of Lisieux had its own tradition long before it was linked to a saint. For hundreds of years the roofs of the old Norman houses have sloped down over their windows like monks' cowls. Though the bombs of World War II wiped out many of the cross-beamed houses, the town still seems to breathe the old ways. The region is famous for bubbly apple cider, restaurants serve homemade onion soup, and the families who run pensions rise early to serve their guests hot croissants. It is easy to imagine a little girl fishing with her father in the river that races cheerily through the center of town, and just as easy to see Thérèse and Louis walking together along the streets. Mornings on his way to work a Mr. Rixe, a notary public, used to pass the aging man walking with his very young daughter. "I just stopped and stared at her," he said, "that little girl with her mass of golden hair."[5]

Quaint Norman architecture did not charm the Martins. Their home was a classic two-story brick building with a backyard in which the metal cage where Louis kept birds still sits like a giant canary cage. It is an irony that here in her own home the real Thérèse fades before the sentiment of the past 50 years or so. Anchored in the backyard where Thérèse played at making mixtures of seeds and bark that she found[6] are two life-sized statues — Thérèse and Louis frozen in white. The child, her face framed with stone ringlets, looks up pleadingly; the man stares off in proud resignation. The place, we are told, is where Thérèse asked her father's permission to enter the convent. The real scene took place only a few weeks after Louis Martin had suffered a slight stroke.[7] When his youngest daughter asked to leave him, his first reaction was to break down and cry.[8]

Pictures rim the bedroom where Thérèse slept with two of her sisters. In one a child — haloed, dressed in white, hands clasped, eyes heavenward — kneels in the grass. The face is chalk white — a porcelain doll at prayer. In the background a gray figure of a man with a white beard and white dress hat sits holding a pole over water. Someone's conception of a saintly child fishing with her father.

Down the hill toward town are the flying buttresses and gargoyles of the Cathedral of Saint Pierre. It, too, has its tradition. The cathedral was begun 800 years ago and seems to have bulged and spread at odd angles over the centuries. One of the chapels was built by Pierre Caucon, a bishop of Lisieux and one of Joan of Arc's judges. Rain has stained the cool stone of the walls and the graceful high arches inside various shades of gray and yellow. But for Thérèse and her sisters and cousins and father and aunt and uncle, who knelt together on Sundays, the focus was not the Gothic arches nor the bleached stone nor even the large stained-glass window above the altar, but the priest. His back to them, bent over the sacramental bread and wine, he whispered the words of consecration in Latin. To the left of the entrance stands a confessional box near a fluted pillar so thick a child couldn't begin to stretch her arms around it. Near this pillar the six and one-half years old Thérèse knelt before she crossed the aisle to slip into the dark box for the first time where the priest waited to hear her confession. St. Pierre is not a monument. It remains very much as it was, only now the Mass is in French and the priest faces the people.

The monument is the mammoth Basilica of Saint Thérèse that rises over the town like the ghost of a great castle. It is, according to the brochure, "one of the biggest churches built in the 20th century"[9] and standing on the terrace dwarfed by the huge dome it is easy to believe. It can accommodate 4,000 people, a hint of the thousands who throng to Lisieux because of her. Such a big church for someone nicknamed the "Little Flower."

In the tomblike crypt of the basilica five large mosaics

3

The Basilica of Saint Thérèse in Lisieux, France

show Thérèse in scenes from birth to death. Upstairs, "Above the west gallery," says the brochure, "the middle panel shows Saint Thérèse surrounded by four Popes who contributed to her glorification."[10] A reliquary in the south transcept contains two bones from her right arm, the idea of Pope Pius XI. The story she wrote of her life affected millions, and Thérèse was right-handed.

There is, it seems, a St. Thérèse for all tastes. Those who prefer theater and spectacle may buy tickets and take their places when the sun goes down for the sound and light show, which the brochure promises will be "a dazzling evocation of Thérèse Martin's life." Images of Thérèse's life flash on two large movie screens while laser beams fracture the light to create sensational effects through smoke floating in the darkened church. As the laser beam slices the smoke the audience hears the panicked voice of a child — a sick Thérèse — call "Mamma."

Below the main church near the crypt is a stark and moving display of the life of a Carmelite nun — with wall-sized photos of veiled, kneeling women. After the plastic souvenirs jamming the open shops in town — a painted nun rimmed in plastic Christmas lights, Thérèse in a bubble of water flecked with artificial snow, Thérèse surrounded with seashells — the life-sized model of Thérèse's room at the monastery with its pine board floor and simple bed covered with a rough tan cloth seems warm and human. This display exists to satisfy the craving of thousands of people who wanted to get past the spectacular monuments and the plastic souvenirs to glimpse the mysterious world in which she lived, but were not allowed in. The Carmel of Lisieux is not a monument, but a functioning monastery.

Those who want to see still more of that mysterious world may watch a 30-minute film made in the early 1960s, "The True Face of Thérèse of Lisieux." At the allotted hour the door of the little theater off the basilica terrace remains locked. Within minutes a gray-haired priest with rosy cheeks, a beret and a movie projector arrives. He unlocks the door, leads visitors into a small room and slips behind a cashier's booth. After small fees are paid, he turns to the projector and starts the film.

In this film is shown the actual cloister door that Thérèse Martin passed through. As the camera approaches we see that the door has no outside handle. It opens, rather eerily, from the inside. The camera passes through and focuses on two figures veiled from head to toe — even the faces. Once the camera is inside, one of the veiled figures closes the door and bolts it top and bottom with old iron bolts, and locks it with a key worthy of the bastille. For a moment this shutting and bolting of that cloister door jolts one free from both plastic images and laser effects into an instant of contact with the real Thérèse. She chose to lock herself up behind that door for life.

Out in the air again, a 10-minute walk down the hill takes the visitor to the Carmel itself — a tidy group of stone buildings sitting on a half moon of a street in the middle of town. In the little reliquary off to the left of the entrance is displayed Thérèse's waist-length thick blond curls — cut off in the monastery and preserved. In the chapel a model of her body in the dress habit of a Carmelite nun, and encased in glass, reclines on a slab of marble. With one hand she clutches a flower, with the other her breast. The glass case is gilded in baroque style. "It used to be surrounded by angels," said a nun, "but they were removed."

Small plaques engraved with little messages literally fill the walls and even the pillars of the chapel — right to the floor. In one form or another the message is the same: Thank you, St. Thérèse. Signed a mother, a Belgian, an Egyptian, a soldier. The echo of the shuffling stops as nuns' voices begin to chant. They still pray the Divine Office in the choir to the right of the altar four times a day — as Thérèse did nearly a hundred years ago.

The baroque "tomb" of St. Thérèse is a reminder that she belonged to a Church with a long tradition. The price of inheriting the wisdom of those who lived in an earlier era is the wrapping — the artistic taste of the ages it passes through. Like grandmother's old flowered housedress, it is not what I would choose, but neither is it the main point. To the left of the chapel lies the sacristy smelling of old candle wax, and inside the sacristy is that metal cloister door, the one that cannot be opened from the outside. It, too, is covered with inscriptions. Just as the angels were removed from her tomb, since the mid-1940s scholars have been slowly peeling away other gilding around St. Thérèse — the touched up photos, the sweet words slipped by other hands into her written memories. When the gilding is all stripped away and she is cleared too of false sentiment, of false mystery, the cloister door with no outside handle remains.

According to Thérèse, one day while she was at school

one of the sisters asked her how she spent her free time.

"I told her I went behind my bed in an empty space which was there, and that it was easy to close myself in with my bed curtain and that I *thought*."

"But what do you think about?" she asked.

"I think about God, about life, about ETERNITY . . . I think!"

The nun laughed and from time to time asked Thérèse if she were "still thinking."[11]

Anton Chekhov, a contemporary of Thérèse's, said the writer's job was not to answer the deep questions of life, "but to depict only who, how and in what circumstances people have spoken or thought about God or pessimism."[12] Thérèse thought about God in the midst of some leftover medieval practices, a Jansenist climate of sin and guilt, and an extended family of well-to-do French Catholics. Through the fragments of her life revealed in letters and memories as she wrote them down, and the letters and memories of those who knew her, we will glimpse not the legendary "Little Flower" but Thérèse Martin. This story explores the real mystery of why the child "with her mass of golden hair" chose to step through the cloister door and what happened to her behind that door. The story begins not in Lisieux, but in Alençon, with the first person to know the unsaintly little Thérèse well, her mother Zélie Martin.

 My little daughter was born yesterday. . . . She was very strong and healthy, they tell me she weighs eight pounds, let's put it at six, that isn't bad. . . . I am very content. However at first I was surprised because I expected to have a boy! I pictured that during the last two months, because I felt her much more strongly than my other babies.[1]

The "other babies" that Zélie Martin bore before Thérèse numbered eight. Zélie was a blunt, buoyant, practical woman, not nearly as delicate as the Alençon lace she made. According to her maid, she would often slip out to "the homes of poor families with a hot meal, bottles of wine, coins worth 40 sous, and nobody knew it except us two."[2] Her zest flowed into every line of the rambling, frank letters she wrote regularly to her younger brother.

"I think you are a fool," Zélie wrote to the 23-year-old Isidore when he was studying medicine in Paris in 1864 and was captivated by a certain Mademoiselle X. "You know that all that glitters is not gold. The principle is to look for a good interior woman, who is not afraid to dirty her hands with work."[3] Zélie had no fear of dirtying her own hands. At the time she wrote this letter she was pregnant with her fourth child in four years, while running a little lace business from her home. Though she farmed out the actual sewing — she employed about 20 women — Zélie kept the accounts and pieced the lace strips together herself.[4] The delicate work gave Zélie "nightmares." "I have a violent headache," she wrote to Isidore in 1865," and am exposed to incessant worries . . . today I have a swollen breast gland that concerns me."[5] The lace made her "a slave of the worst slavery."[6]

Zélie faced more painful nightmares during the six years just prior to Thérèse's birth. She already worried about her third child, Léonie, who suffered convulsions and had eczema so badly that at times it covered her body.[7] In the winter of 1867 the Martin's first son, Joseph, died at the age of five months. The next year a second son, a second Joseph, died at eight months. After five days of vomiting, the baby lived a last night of such "cruel suffering" that Zélie prayed for him to die.[8] In the spring of 1869 Zélie bore another child, and now she was plainly frightened. She wrote her brother and sister-in-law. "I have had, already, torments for this child. I sense that I will wear myself down. I have the impression that I will not live a long time." Often she ran a fever.[9]

The next winter it was not the baby, Céline, who grew ill, but Hélène, five and one-half years old. This time Zélie faced a torturous doubt. Her doctor advised her to feed the child bouillon with a little rice or barley. Over the weekend, when Hélène could not swallow the hearty bouillon, Zélie followed her maid's suggestion of bread soaked in water. Hélène ate the bread soup, not as nourishing as bouillon, on Saturday and Sunday. By Monday morning when the doctor finally saw the child she had a congested lung and mild typhoid fever. She must, the doctor stressed, have bouillon. That night Zélie once more held a dying child. She wrote Isidore about feeding Hélène the light soup. "My dear brother, do you think that is what made her die?"[10]

In August, six months after Hélène died, Zélie could not nurse the newest baby, called Thérèse. She sent the child to the home of a wet nurse, and by October this baby, too, was dead. "If you knew what happened to my poor little Thérèse, she wrote her brother. "Her vile wet nurse made her die of starvation."[11] Zélie had suspected nothing, but the doctor told her the child had "fasted." He had, he said, been able to count her bones. Now, despite her own poor health and the death of four children in four years Zélie wanted one more child and this child she was determined not to lose. "I do not want a little boy, but a little Thérèse who resembles her, and who will not go with a wet-nurse (for this time I will take a wet nurse into my home). No, never, if the good God grants me other children they will not leave the house."[12]

Thus the 41-year-old Zélie's delighted announcement of the birth of her ninth child in January of 1873, baptized, at the age of two days, Marie Françoise Thérèse Martin. The delight dimmed quickly. Two weeks later Thérèse developed an intestinal illness. "I notice the same alarming symptoms," Zélie wrote her brother, " as my other babies who died."[13] Zélie continued to try to nurse Thérèse herself until one March evening when the doctor warned her to find a wet nurse immediately if she wanted to save the child.[14]

With Louis away on a trip, Zélie watched through the night alone. Thérèse was unable to drink. At daybreak Zélie left the house to walk about four miles along the deserted roads and open farmlands of the countryside to a small, plain, stone farmhouse. She begged Rose Taillé, a 37-year-old farmer's wife who had nursed the two dead boys, to come back to town with her. By the time the two women walked back to the Martin house the baby looked so feeble that Rose just shook her head. Still she lifted the baby to her breast and nursed her, and Thérèse clung to Rose until one o'clock that afternoon, breathing so softly that Zélie thought she was dead. Thérèse was still alive, but Rose, with children of her own, could not stay at the Martin house for more than a week. Once again Zélie sent a child off to live with someone else.[15]

When Thérèse came to visit her family in May, she was healthy enough to keep up a lusty cry until she was carried to the market to stay with Rose while she sold her butter.[16] By the time Thérèse was six months old the nearly perpetual cloud of infant death had lifted from the Martin household. Zélie wrote to her second oldest daughter, Pauline, who was away at school, about Thérèse's latest visit. "The little one did nothing but laugh . . . one would say she already wants to play, so that will come soon. She holds herself up on her two little legs straight as a post. I believe she will walk very early. . . . She appears very intelligent and has the face of a little cherub."[17]

That summer Thérèse grew fat, healthy and quite tanned. Rose wheeled her out into the fields on a pile of hay.[18] Now Thérèse never cried. She learned to crawl in the stone cottage and then walk about the open flat fields of Rose Taillé's farm to visit the cow, Roussette, and to pick wild flowers. At 15 months Thérèse came home for good, and she was, in the pleasantly biased view of her mother, "a charming child . . . very sweet and very advanced for her age."[19] Before she turned three Thérèse was starting to read. Now Zélie's letters rang with the news of a healthy child about the house, a normal child with "a stubborn streak."

> As for the little imp, one doesn't know how things will go, she is so small, so thoughtless! Her intelligence is superior to Céline's, but she's less gentle and has a stubborn streak in her that is almost invincible; when she says "no" nothing can make her give in, and one could put her in the cellar a whole day and she'd sleep there rather than say "yes." But still she has a heart of gold; she is very lovable and frank. . . .[20]

The "little imp" also threw "frightful tantrums" and banged her head against her wooden bed.[21] These first years Thérèse later dubbed "the sunny years." They did pass nearly unclouded, with one exception. When Thérèse was three and a half Zélie wrote her brother that for some months the child had an unnatural "oppression." "When she walks a little quickly, one can hear something like a strange whistle in her chest. . . . My God, if I lost this child what sadness I would have! And my husband adores her!"[22]

It was Zélie's life, not the baby's, that was in danger. Christmas that year (1876) her doctor told her that a breast tumor was beyond the help of surgery. She wrote to Isidore, who now owned a pharmacy in Lisieux, and he quickly arranged for Zélie to consult a surgeon there. Christmas Eve found Zélie writing to her husband from Lisieux. "Doctor Notta finds it very regrettable that they did not operate at the beginning, but now it is too late."[23] Zélie had first mentioned the troublesome breast gland 11 years earlier.

At first only Louis knew the truth, and the truth shattered him. Louis Martin was a gentle, quiet man raised in the strictness of French military camps. He tried to spend his life as a monk in the Swiss Alps, but did not know Latin, so Louis lived with his parents and became a watchmaker. The pieces of his day, beginning at 5:30 a.m. with Mass, fit as carefully as those of the watches he made. When he did marry at age 35 he suggested to his 26-year-old bride, Zélie (who had once wanted to be a nun), a union without physical love. Until a priest intervened 10 months after the wedding, there was none. As the years passed Louis leaned more and more on his strong-willed wife. Zélie ran the home while Louis went on pilgrimages. Zélie nursed the sick children. And Zélie's lace business became so profitable by 1870 that Louis gave up his watchmaking to manage her affairs.[24] When he heard the news of his wife's incurable cancer Louis was "like one destroyed."[25]

Zélie was not. She believed, in realistic terms, in the faith she had lived. Often she had spoken of the homeland, the next life. Though she prayed and hoped for a miracle, she began to prepare Marie and Pauline to take her place. She prepared them calmly. "The little ones don't disturb me," she wrote Pauline, "since both of them are very good; they are special, and certainly will turn out well. You and Marie will be able to raise them perfectly. Céline never commits the smallest deliberate fault. The little one will be all right too, for she wouldn't tell a lie for all the gold in the world, and she has a spirit about her which I have not seen in any of you."[26]

"All the details of my mother's illness are still present to me," Thérèse wrote 18 years later, "and I recall especially the last weeks she spent on earth. Céline and I were like two poor little exiles, for every morning Madame Leriche came to get us and brought us to her home where we spent the day."[27] In August, as the end drew near, Thérèse and Céline were brought into the small room with their sisters to stand around their mother's bed for the final anointing. "I can still see the spot where I was by Céline's side. All five of us were lined up according to age, and Papa was there too, sobbing. . . ."

I don't recall having cried very much, neither did I speak to anyone about the feelings I experienced. I looked and listened in silence. No one had any time to pay any attention to me, and I saw many things they would have hidden from me . . . once I was standing before the lid of the coffin which had been placed upright in the hall. I stopped for a long time gazing at it. Though I'd never seen one before I understood what it was. I was so little that in spite of Mama's small stature, I had to *raise* my head to take in its full height. It appeared *large* and *dismal*.[28]

When Zélie was laid out Louis hoisted Thérèse up over the coffin and leaned her down to kiss her dead mother's forehead. The "sunny years" had ended.

Lost, the 54-year-old Louis listened to the Guérins'

idea to sell the business and move to Lisieux where Isidore and his wife Céline could help raise the girls. Isidore moved quickly. Two weeks after Zélie's death the grieving Louis received a letter from his brother-in-law describing in elaborate detail the house he had found, "capable of lodging seven . . . in a healthful section . . . with a garden or, at least, a little flower bed for the children." The house had four bedrooms, two dressing rooms, a belvedere complete with fireplace, "three attics well-lighted and papered," a fruit and wine cellar. He even described the "carriage gateway for bringing in provisions (wood, cider) . . . a very comfortable shelter for poultry and rabbits, an enclosure with a shelter and a bath for ducks, etc. etc." and a water pump.[29] Isidore was precise. The house, he reported, was exactly 700 paces from the Church, and 764 paces from his own house.[30] Isidore was also energetic, explosive, a member by marriage of Lisieux's richest family, a militant royalist, an anti-Semite,[31] and now deputy guardian of the five Martin girls.[32]

Less than three months after their mother's death, dressed in black mourning dresses, the girls prayed at Zélie's grave one last time before boarding the train with their Uncle Isidore. Four hours later the train eased into the little station in their new hometown of Lisieux.[33] The girls quickly nicknamed their new home "Les Buissonnets," the little bushes. With Zélie gone life was quieter than in Alençon. Sunday evenings that winter the small kitchen glowed with the fire while Louis sang little songs or recited poems with Thérèse and Céline on his knees, "rocking us gently."[34]

The world of a small child who has lost her mother hinges less on the charm of a house or the charm of a town than on the adults surrounding her. The Martin family knew no one in Lisieux except the Guérins. Each Sunday the girls, attired properly in dresses and lace collars, joined their Uncle Isidore and Aunt Céline and cousins Jeanne and Marie for Mass at the grand Cathedral of

14

Saint-Pierre. Some Sunday evenings Thérèse spent with one of her sisters at the Guérins'. "I listened with great pleasure to all Uncle had to say, but I didn't like it when he asked me questions. I was very much frightened when he placed me on his knee and sang 'Blue Beard' in a formidable tone of voice. I was happy to see Papa coming to fetch us."[35]

As in Zélie's time, Louis' life remained regulated. He spent his time reading up in the belvedere or in his room, tending the birds in his backyard aviary, off on fishing trips or pilgrimages.[36] Though he did not actively raise Thérèse, he provided a stable, kind influence and a prominent part of his afternoon ritual involved his blonde, blue-eyed "little queen." The oldest and the youngest in the family grew closer. Together the two explored the town with its tanneries and spinning mills, cloth factories, military barracks, and sloping streets lined with old Norman houses.[37] Together they fished in the countryside, where Thérèse loved the flowers and birds and listened "to distant sounds, the murmuring of the wind . . . the indistinct notes of some military music."[38] Together they visited the different churches and together they entered the chapel of the Carmelite monastery, an easy half-hour walk down the hill from home if they took their time. There Louis pointed out to Thérèse a dark metal grill on the right side of the altar behind which, he said, knelt the nuns. The pair seemed so contented that Thérèse appeared free of scars from her mother's death. The scars were there, but carved in too deeply to be seen.

"I wasn't even able to think of Papa *dying* without trembling," she recalled. One day when she stood below him while he was on a ladder, he told her to move; "if I fall, I'll crush you!" Thérèse felt "an interior revulsion" and grasped the ladder.[39] One afternoon when Thérèse was six or seven and playing alone in the attic while her father was off on a trip, she glanced out into the garden.

> ... I saw a man dressed exactly like Papa
> standing in front of the laundry. ... The man
> had the same height and walk as Papa, only he
> was *much more stooped*. His *head* was cov-
> ered with a sort of apron of indistinct color and
> it hid his face. He wore a hat similar to Papa's. I
> saw him walking at a regular pace ... surely
> Papa had returned and was hiding to surprise
> me; then I called out very loudly: "Papa!
> Papa!" ... But the mysterious personage, ap-
> pearing not to hear, continued his steady pace
> without even turning around. ... I saw him go
> toward the grove which divides the wide path in
> two, and I waited to see him reappear on the oth-
> er side of the tall trees, but ... (he) had van-
> ished! ...[40]

Marie rushed in. Victoire the maid must have been
teasing, she reassured Thérèse. She probably hid her face
in her apron. But Victoire was still in the kitchen. They
found no one in the garden. Louis had not come home.[41]

Though she loved her father and other sisters, after
her mother's death Thérèse fixed her heart on Pauline. It
was Pauline's bed she crawled into when she was sick;
Pauline who eased her fear of the dark by sending her on
errands to far rooms of the house; Pauline who gave permission even for walks with her father. Pauline set up a
series of classes for her sole pupil and gave grades. Long
before the modern behaviorist trend, she assigned Thérèse
points to exchange for a prize or a day out of school.[42] Finally, it was Pauline's lap that Thérèse climbed onto to
hear stories of God, and Pauline "who received all my intimate confidences and cleared up all my doubts."[43]

At six and a half Thérèse prepared to receive the Sacrament of Penance. The penitent passed alone into a darkened confessional box, separated from the priest by a
wooden partition, and whispered his or her sins. Though

16

theology stressed forgiveness and grace, for some the conditions of confession provoked fear. What the teenaged Pauline said and the tone in which she said it formed Thérèse's attitude toward her first confession. Pauline spoke of love and gratitude — Thérèse seemed to her an obviously good child. In the baroque language of French Catholicism, Pauline told Thérèse that when she went to confession "the tears of the Child Jesus would fall on her soul and purify it at the moment of the priest's blessing."[44] She did not emphasize sin or guilt.

On the day of her first confession Thérèse climbed the steps of the cathedral and knelt near the back. Everywhere were arches and angles and bleached gray stone. When her turn came she slipped into her side of the dark wood confessional box and knelt down. Abbé Ducellier opened the grate and found no one there. "I was so little my head was below the arm rest. He told me to stand up. Obeying instantly, I stood and faced him directly in order to see him perfectly, and I made my confession like *a big girl*." Thérèse bounded out of the confessional box "happy and light-hearted."[45]

Inevitably the day came when Thérèse stepped out of the warm world of Pauline and into a Catholic girls' school. Dressed in the dark uniform with its white collar and green belt, her hair freshly curled into long ringlets, Thérèse kissed Pauline good-bye and walked each morning with her sister Céline and her cousins to the old buildings with their older tradition — the Benedictine Abbey of Notre-Dame-du-Pré — to spend "the saddest years of my life."[46]

Thérèse was eight and a half when she started school and she quickly became an outcast. To the nuns she was the child who cried constantly because she had lost her mother. To the other girls she was the coddled child with fancy ringlets.[47] But since she recited her lessons well, the second year she was placed in a class above her age, provoking the jealousy of an older classmate. The children

17

mocked her, tousled her curls. Alone during recreation, Thérèse "walked sick and sad in the big yard."[48] The paradoxical effect of school was to thrust her more deeply into her family. She played with Céline and her cousin Marie, three years older.

Thérèse and Marie played a unique game — they were hermits with "nothing but a poor hut, a little garden where they grew corn and other vegetables."[49] The game was rooted in a serious plan. Thérèse dreamed of a day when she would go to live alone with Pauline in a far-off desert beyond schools and other people, and told her secret dream to Pauline. "She answered that my desire was also hers and that she *was waiting* for me to be big enough for her to leave."[50] To Thérèse the casual words constituted a sealed promise. No matter how painful school became, later she would share her life with Pauline.

By accident Thérèse overheard Pauline tell Marie her real plans — to enter the Carmelite monastery in Lisieux. Since the Carmelites were cloistered, once Pauline left home she would never come back, not for a visit, not for grave illness, not even for a death. ". . . having heard about it by surprise, it was if a sword were buried in my heart . . . I didn't know what Carmel was, but I understood that Pauline was going to leave me to enter a convent. I understood too, that she *would not wait for me*, and I was about to lose my second *Mother*! . . . In one instant, I understood what life was . . . nothing but a continual suffering and separation."[51] By the end of that painful day Thérèse had linked the Carmel to the desert of her dreams.

Pauline left home in October on the first day of school. Early that morning Thérèse kissed her good-bye at home, went to Mass with her cousins, cried, and went to school. Later her aunt took the girls to the Carmel where Thérèse saw a sight that seared into her memory — "*my Pauline* behind the *grille*."[52] She might have adjusted more easily
18

if she had been totally cut off from Pauline, but each Thursday the family paraded down the hill to the Carmel to visit — for a total of one half hour. When the Guérins came, out of courtesy Pauline spoke with them. Other days Marie ate up the half hour talking to her sister. Once, to gain attention, Thérèse pointed out to Pauline that she was wearing the skirt she had made for her.[53] Pauline took little notice. Week after week Thérèse was left with only a couple of minutes alone with Pauline at the end of the visit. "I spent . . . (the time) in crying and left with a broken heart. I didn't understand . . . and I said in the depths of my heart: 'Pauline is lost to me.' "[54] Before long Thérèse developed headaches.

At Easter Louis Martin took Marie and Léonie to Paris, leaving Céline and Thérèse with the Guérins. One evening her uncle, of whom Thérèse was always a bit frightened, took her for a walk and reminisced about her mother. Thérèse started to cry. Calling her softhearted, her uncle tried to distract her by chattering of the good times they planned. That night as she got ready for bed Thérèse began to tremble. "Believing I was cold, Aunt covered me with blankets and surrounded me with hot water bottles. But nothing was able to stop my shaking, which lasted all night."[55]

The chills became hallucinations, seizures, paralysis. Thérèse's cousin Jeanne remembered "propulsive seizures during which she made wheel-like movements that she would have been absolutely incapable of making in a state of health."[56] "She had terrifying dreams," Marie said, ". . . some nails fixed in the wall of the room suddenly became as thick, charred fingers to her . . . her eyes, usually so calm and so kindly, had a terror-stricken expression. . . ."[57] Thérèse also flung herself on the floor with "extraordinary force."[58] "I often appeared to be in a faint," Thérèse later recalled, "not making the slightest movement . . . yet I heard everything that was said around me. . . ."[59]

There was no doubt in Marie's mind that this was the work of the devil, who "even tried to kill our little sister. Her bed was in a big alcove, and there was a space between wall and bed at both ends; she used to try and throw herself into this space. Several times she succeeded, and I wonder how she did not split her head on the paving-stones . . . other times she would bang her head against the wood of the bedstead. And there were times when she tried to speak to me, but no sound could be heard."[60]

The family called in Dr. Notta, the same man who had told Zélie Martin her tumor was inoperable. The illness baffled the doctor. His comments did nothing to relieve the fears of the family. Perhaps, he thought, it was St. Vitus's dance, or "hysteria," a common diagnosis of women at the time, but he had never seen it in a child. Dr. Notta "gave the impression," Jeanne Guérin said, "that there was more to it than just that. Just what, he did not know himself; if he had known he would have told my father."[61] According to Marie, "One day the doctor was present during one of these attacks, and he said to my father: 'Science is powerless before these phenomena: there is nothing to be done.' "[62] Isidore Guérin connected Thérèse's condition to dreaming about Pauline and grew furious one day when he came into the room and found Thérèse with her doll dressed as a Carmelite nun.[63] As for poor Louis Martin, he was simply helpless, believing, Thérèse later said, that *"his little girl was going crazy or was about to die."*[64]

While Thérèse appeared delirious she apparently remained lucid, aware of what was going on around her throughout the six weeks of the illness. Marie noticed that she could coax Thérèse to eat — "she was missing a tooth and I said. . . . 'It doesn't bother me that your teeth are clenched. I'll be able to feed you some bouillon through that little hole'. . . . Immediately her teeth were unclenched."[65] Thérèse herself believed she *"was not deprived of the use of my reason for one single instant."* She observed her visitors *"seated around my bed LIKE A ROW OF ONIONS, looking at me as though I were a strange beast."*[66]

As reports of seizures and clenched teeth flowed down the hill to the Carmel, Pauline reacted with less terror and with less patience than those around Thérèse's bed. "I am a little angry with you," she wrote Thérèse, "almost very angry. . . . If I were holding you in my arms, I would have to watch over myself to refrain from choking you."[67] She was scheduled to go through the solemn ceremony of receiving the Carmelite habit on April 6th — a ceremony similar to a wedding. For the last time in her life Pauline could step out of the cloister and rejoin her family, and she wanted Thérèse there. "Come now, Miss Bather, Miss Trembler, Miss Feverish, Miss Sleepyhead, Miss Drinker, you must not plan on carrying on all these titles of a grubby and fishy nobility here on Friday."[68]

Pauline's gambit worked — but only for the day. Thérèse went to the Carmel and saw her sister come into the chapel dressed as a bride, then return to the cloister to don the robes of a nun. The next day Thérèse had a relapse that continued for weeks. As she had when teaching Thérèse as a young child, Pauline resorted to clever psychology. Early in May she dangled before Thérèse a long private party with just the two of them — to take place when Thérèse was cured. "Our mother (the Prioress) has promised me that I'll see the *cured little one* in the . . . speakroom . . . we'll stay there, the two of us, as long as we want. . . . We'll babble and babble and laugh, and it will be a case of who outdoes the other."[69]

On a Sunday in mid-May Léonie, taking her turn in the sickroom, was reading by the window. She ignored Thérèse's constant moaning — "Mama, Mama," meaning Marie. Thérèse's voice grew louder and the calls for "Mama" built to such a pitch that Marie burst into the room frightened and found Thérèse struggling so hard that Marie thought she would die. Thérèse didn't recognize

21

Marie. When she tried to give her a drink Thérèse thought it was poison. Frantic, Marie knelt by a statue of the Virgin Mary and pleaded for her sister's life. She watched Thérèse "fix her gaze on the statue," grow calm, and begin to cry quietly. The symptoms vanished.[70]

A vision, thought Marie, a miraculous cure. When they were alone Marie pressed her sister to tell what she had seen. The Virgin Mary, said Thérèse, had smiled at her. Marie rushed the story down to the Carmel and soon Thérèse was down there too, ringed with excited nuns and peppered with questions. How much light was there? Was the Blessed Virgin alone or holding the Child Jesus? Despite the press of their expectations, Thérèse repeated exactly what she believed she had seen. "The Blessed Virgin had appeared *very beautiful*, and I had seen her *smile at me*."[71] That was all.

It was not quite enough for the Carmelites, falling short of their picture of a vision. The nuns had "imagined something else entirely." Still Thérèse held to her simple description of the Virgin's smile. She did not polish her story, but the subdued circle of nuns shook her confidence. "I thought I had lied." Self-doubt poisoned Thérèse until she doubted even whether she had been truly ill. Perhaps she had only pretended the seizures, the hallucinations. "I was unable to look upon myself without a feeling of *profound horror*."[72] She was 10 years old.

The year following her illness Thérèse, still emotionally fragile, was preparing for the major religious event of her childhood — her First Communion, the Sacrament of the Eucharist.[73] As a very small child she had heard that the host the priest would place on her tongue one day was no mere symbolic piece of bread but the real body and blood of Jesus Christ. Now Marie spoke more to her of spiritual things, of "the way of becoming *holy* through fidelity in little things."[74] At school Thérèse spent her recesses memorizing her catechism to recite for the Abbé

Domin. The impulse was competitive — she wanted to be first and cried if she forgot a word. "I grasped easily the meaning of the things I was learning, but I had trouble learning things word for word."[75] She placed first.

During the months of preparation Marie held Thérèse on her lap and taught her about holiness; the nuns and the abbé at school trained her in the catechism; but it was Pauline who shaped her image of the sacrament. Each week Pauline wrote to Thérèse wrapping her thoughts in the language of naturalistic imagery and sweetness — "for little girls very good, very sweet, very diligent today, the Holy Child in the crib reserves all kinds of divine caresses. . . . I trust . . . that you may merit these caresses by very many efforts and by love."[76] Beneath the embroidered words lay a clear message — to prepare to receive Christ within her, Thérèse must show God her love by her efforts. As Lent approached, when the Carmelites kept a strict ban on mail, Pauline asked the Prioress for an exception to continue writing to Thérèse.

Pauline required no memorizing. She decorated a copy book for Thérèse to write down her sacrifices, good deeds, acts of love. These Pauline called flowers. Letters flowed from the Carmel filled with images of gardens, soil, the sun's warmth, roses, lilies. "Do you know, my darling, that your flowers need warmth in order to bloom? Well your love will be the sweet sun that will make them bloom under the feet of Jesus."[77] Thérèse dutifully totaled up her brief prayers in Pauline's notebook. "Little Jesus, I love You." (50) "Little Jesus I kiss you." (50) By the day of her First Communion Thérèse had recorded a grand total of 2,773 such prayers and 818 sacrifices.[78]

Such anticipation may portend an anticlimax, but on the day of Thérèse's First Communion the opposite occurred. She said she experienced the Eucharist as "a fusion." "I *felt* that I *was loved*. . . . There were no demands made, no struggles, no sacrifices."[79] The celebrations of the day ended that evening at the Carmel. Pauline had received permission to make her profession, final vows for life, on the day of Thérèse's First Communion. That evening Thérèse's dream took on a more concrete shape. "There I saw my *Pauline* . . . with her white veil, one like mine, and her crown of roses. . . . I hoped to be with her soon and to await *heaven* with her!"[80]

Thérèse passed the year after her First Communion calmly, and in May moved into the abbey for a few days of spiritual retreat. During her initial retreat at the abbey before her First Communion the nuns treated Thérèse cautiously, sending her for air or rest if she coughed or even looked pale. Her nervous family visited her each night with treats.[81] Despite the "cure" of the year before, she was still treated as a sickly child. But that retreat had gone well. A year later, isolated, Thérèse heard another side of French Catholicism, the side linked to Jansenism. Pauline's teaching of love, personal sacrifice and the symbol of flowers was now pitted against the Abbé Domin. He reminded his young audience that they would die, that one of them might die before the end of the retreat. "What the abbé told us was frightening. He spoke about mortal sin, and he described a soul in the state of sin and how much God hated it. He compared it to a little dove soaked in mud, and who is no longer able to fly."[82] Mortal sins must be confessed. The abbé told the girls that to receive Communion without confessing mortal sins was a sacrilege.

The priest's words plunged Thérèse into terror about the state of her own soul — "for me to express what I suffered *for a year and a half* would be impossible. All my most simple thoughts and actions became the cause of trouble for me."[83] Significant here is the word "thoughts." Marie's personality could be smothering. Any thoughts less than purely kind about Marie caused Thérèse torment. And Thérèse was age 12, the age when young girls become aware of new emotions and of changes within their bodies. Consenting to impure thoughts was considered sinful.[84]

24

Thérèse wanted Pauline. But this time Pauline was powerless to help, for Thérèse needed someone close at hand to whom she could pour out her terror. Between her and Pauline were "impassable walls."

> . . . I ended up by recognizing the sad reality: Pauline is lost to me, almost in the same manner as if she were dead. She always loved me, prayed for me, but in my eyes *my* dear *Pauline* had become a saint who was no longer able to understand the things of earth. And the miseries of her poor Thérèse . . . would only astonish her and prevent her from loving her Thérèse as much as she did. And so, in reality, I had only Marie. . . .[85]

While Marie curled Thérèse's hair in the afternoons after school Thérèse cried and poured out to her the deadly sins she believed had tainted her soul. Having gone through this torment herself, Marie called the terror by name — scruples. Scruples were fears, not sins, that came from a distorted sense that normal thoughts and actions were evil. Marie had gone to a retreat three years earlier preached by a 42-year-old Jesuit, Father Pichon, who was said to have "put back in the attic the God of the Jansenists."[86] Marie had opened her soul to this man who wrote her later that year to "forget the malcontent God and see the indulgent God, full of love."[87] Now Marie treated Thérèse's scruples firmly — and when they erupted on the eve of her confession Marie told her exactly what, and what not, to tell the priest. Thérèse listened to her. Despite the abbé's warning that to conceal a deadly sin meant sacrilege, she never told the priest her fear that her thoughts and actions were mortally sinful.[88] But she did become more dependent on Marie. That autumn Céline and Marie Guérin were gone from the abbey and Thérèse went back alone. The scruples persisted; the loneliness persisted. The abbé spoke once again of sin, judgment and hell.[89] During the second term Thérèse fell ill, and this time she left the abbey for good.

Thérèse's formal education was now restricted to the tutoring, several hours a week at most,[90] by Madame Papineau, a woman "a little old-maidish in her ways" who lived with her mother and her cat. Madame Papineau's antique furniture reflected well the atmosphere of the house. While Thérèse studied, her tutor's mother entertained "priests, ladies, young girls. . . ."[91] With many hours of the day at home, Thérèse withdrew into the attic that Pauline had once used for painting. She decorated the attic with a black wood cross, a basket of herbs and flowers, a cage filled with noisy birds, a white desk, statues, flowers, and "the portrait of *Pauline* at the age of ten."[92] Alone in Pauline's attic, Thérèse felt content.

The Guérins invited Thérèse to vacation with them that summer at Trouville. Thérèse's first sight of the sea at age seven had thrilled her, and she had gone with the Guérins to Trouville before and bought fresh fish from the fishermen in port, ridden the ferryboat, explored the narrow streets where fashionable people spent their time at the spas, fished for eels, and sketched buildings and flowers.[93] The days at the sea were active, stimulating, and healthy. But this time Céline did not go along. Alone with the Guérins Thérèse fell sick within a couple of days and came home to her attic world. That summer Marie announced that she, too, would quit the family to enter the Carmel that had swallowed up Pauline. Marie — "the only support which attached me to life!"[94]

Throughout her blighted childhood Thérèse was forming judgments not only from what she was taught, but also from what she saw and experienced firsthand, and she trusted her own judgments. Her uncle may have considered her "a little dunce, good and sweet, and with right judgment, yes, but incapable and clumsy."[95] But at school she learned she was bright. At Madame Papineau's house, and at the Carmel, and on the beach at Trouville people sometimes flattered her, said she was pretty. But Pauline and her father shunned such flattery, as if there were a danger in it.[96]

By the time she heard of Marie's decision to leave home Thérèse already viewed life as "suffering and separation." She found contentment only in the world of things she had created in the attic. The impact of Marie's news was to yank her out of this attic world to yet another judgment. "I resolved to take no pleasure out of earth's attractions. . . . When I learned of Marie's departure my *room* lost its attraction for me."[97] She clung to Marie. She could not pass Marie's door without knocking to see if she could hold her.

As the family journeyed one last time to their hometown of Alençon, Thérèse was once again crying over trivial things. The visit to her mother's grave brought tears because she had left behind a bouquet of cornflowers.[98] And there was an unexpected upset. The 23-year-old Léonie, the child whose eczema, convulsions and poor development had worried Zélie so, walked with her father over to the convent of the Poor Clares in Alençon and, without his knowing it, requested admission. They accepted her on the spot. When her father and sisters saw her again she was clothed in the habit. The sight of the stark, poor convent caused Thérèse a *"contraction of my heart."*[99] A week later Marie left home and Thérèse reacted predictably. "I don't want my darling to cry like this," Marie wrote in November, "but I want her to be good and reasonable. After all, we shouldn't say that today was the last time in her life that she was seeing me!"[100] Early in December Léonie, embarrassed, her hair cut off, broken out with eczema, slipped back into Les Buissonnets.[101] As Christmas approached Thérèse was trapped in a cheerless household. She was turning in a "very narrow circle . . . without knowing how to come out."[102] No day symbolizes more the innocence, delight and trust of childhood. In France it was the custom for children to place their shoes by the fireplace for the Father of Christmas to fill. At midnight on Christmas Eve the people of Lisieux could see from a distance the glowing rose windows of the Cathedral of Saint-Pierre; they could hear the organ music. The Mass was long and filled with the old Latin hymns, and it was the middle of the night when Louis Martin stepped out of the cold to take off his coat in the small kitchen. He noticed Thérèse's shoes alone by the fire. As she climbed the back steps to the second floor he said, wearily, "Well, fortunately, this will be the last year."[103]

The words were not very sharp, but they cut Thérèse. They also shook her to a new realization. It wearied her father to treat her as the child she still was. "Forcing back my tears, I descended the stairs rapidly; controlling the poundings of my heart, I took my slippers and placed them in front of Papa, and withdrew all the objects joyfully. . . . Papa was laughing."[104] Thérèse made a simple choice. Despite the sudden emptiness of the ritual, she would conceal her feelings in order to give her father pleasure. In the act of opening her Christmas shoes — the symbol of childhood — Thérèse realized that she was no longer a child. During that Christmas Eve she experienced what she called a "conversion." To her this incident marked, paradoxically, the return of "the strength of soul which she had lost at the age of four and a half."[105]

THE CAMPAIGN

*The Imitation of Christ* was printed by hand in a monk's cell long before the fine leather-bound editions took their places next to the Bible and the Latin missal on the bookshelves of literate Catholics. By the time Thérèse opened the book in the winter of 1887 she had begun to breathe new air. With her scruples cleared away, her torment stilled, the words seemed to describe her own trapped existence and to offer a pathway out. Thérèse read Thomas à Kempis not with intellectual distance, but as if he had traced each letter for her.

> Great trust should not be put in a frail and mortal man, even though he be useful and dear to us; neither ought we to be much grieved if sometimes he cross and contradict us. They that today are with thee tomorrow may be against thee: and often do they veer right round like the wind.[1]

Detach yourself, said Thomas, from all things and all people. "Why doest thou look around thee here; since this is not the place of thy rest? . . . All things pass: and thou with them. Beware thou cling not: lest thou be caught and perish."[2] The one who seeks peace must shun fretfulness, shun anxiety, shun human familiarity and embrace solitude and silence. "The Kingdom of God is within you. . . . Turn thee with thy whole heart unto the Lord;

29

and forsake this wretched world: and thy soul shall find rest."[3]

Thérèse tucked the book in her muff in the winter and in her pocket in the summer and read and reread it until the Guérins could open *The Imitation of Christ* to any page and listen to Thérèse recite it by heart. She felt that the words of Thomas "nourished" her like "pure flour." Most of his words, that is. For Thérèse resisted one significant piece of Thomas à Kempis' advice — his caution against the folly of "vain and secular knowledge." With a surge of energy as if a fever had broken, Thérèse launched out on her own and began to read — mainly history and science. "The other studies left me indifferent, but these two subjects attracted all my attention; in a few months I acquired more knowledge than during my years of study. . . . The chapter in the *Imitation* which speaks of *knowledge* came frequently to my mind, but I found ways of continuing all the same, telling myself that being at an age for studying, it could not be bad to do it."[4] As a rule Thérèse did not read her father's books, but when she found one entitled *End of the Present World and the Mysteries of the Future Life* by Abbé Arminjon, she asked to read it.

This book reflected not the quiet authority of one who had spent years painstakingly recording truths gleaned from his own monastic life, but the didactic certitude of the late 19th century, an age which preferred its views wrapped in the mantle of science. The views of Abbé Arminjon were a mixture of traditional Catholic beliefs about God, and fundamentalism. "The world will have an end. It is a fact certain and without doubt." The final judgment would take place after the appearance of the Antichrist, who would be Jewish. Hell was located at the center of the earth.[5] But Thérèse skimmed past the scientism to the heart of the message — that man was a traveler to an eternal life and earth only his bark, a notion that fit with her own emerging view of life. Abbé Arminjon de-

30

picted that other life as the vision of God. Seeing God "face to face" awaited those "who love Him, (not with the eye but with the heart)," Thérèse wrote later, "and seeing the eternal rewards had no proportion to life's small sacrifices, I wanted *to love, to love Jesus with a passion.*"[6]

Her reading fed a growing inner life, for Thérèse practiced her own form of interior prayer. To belong to the children of Mary, an organization that all the Martin girls had joined, she was required to spend two afternoons a week at the abbey "to prove my worthiness." With no one to talk to she spent her empty afternoons in the chapel in front of the tabernacle sitting alone for a long period in the presence of the consecrated host.[7] Christ became more tangible to her than the nuns and the girls chatting in the courtyard. By May Thérèse had received permission from her confessor, 34-year-old Father Lepelletier, to receive Communion four times a week, a rare privilege during that era in France.[8]

As she grew taller and behaved more maturely, Thérèse graduated from family baby to Céline's confidante. On spring nights the girls climbed into the belvedere to confide their secrets to each other and whisper of the mystery of heaven as they "beheld the white moon rising quietly behind the tall trees, the silvery rays it was casting upon sleeping nature, the bright stars twinkling in the deep skies."[9] In this romantic springtime life held no uncertainty or pain, only beauty, mystery, bliss. Céline and Thérèse were St. Monica and St. Augustine "at the port of Ostia . . . lost in ecstasy at the sight of the Creator's marvels! Doubt was impossible, faith and hope were unnecessary, and *Love* made us find on earth the One whom we were seeking."[10] During those warm nights in the belvedere Thérèse concealed one secret from Céline. Her dream was taking a definite shape. The pull was strong and immediate "To where He waited for me — Him I knew so well."[11] The girl who reacted to the convent school with headaches decided to enter the much stricter Carmel of

Lisieux. What's more, her plan included a definite deadline — she would celebrate the anniversary of her "conversion" behind the Carmel's walls — that Christmas. ". . . the Divine call was so strong that had I been forced to *pass through flames* I would have done it."[12]

Thérèse announced her decision first to Marie and Pauline. Marie would not hear of it. Even though Thérèse was now nearly 5'4" tall — the tallest of the Martin girls — to Marie she remained "always a baby." Pauline was not shocked by the news, only surprised at the timing. At first she withheld encouragement to test Thérèse. But Pauline believed sincerely in the idea of vocation, the "call" from God. For a woman to cut herself off from the ordinary pleasures of life, to drape her body in thick dark wool, and devote her day to prayer, to work, to fasting in the stark cloister made sense only if one had a vocation, and Pauline believed that Thérèse had such a call. Some history lay behind her belief.

After Thérèse overheard Pauline telling Marie about her plan to enter Carmel — five years earlier — Pauline spent some time explaining to Thérèse what Carmel was. For the nine-year-old, Pauline's words somehow connected the desert of her games where she planned to live in the future with the Carmel. She wanted to enter too — an understandable reaction in a child. Pauline took Thérèse to meet the prioress, Mother Marie de Gonzague, an aristocratic, intelligent woman, clever at conversation, with a regal bearing that compensated for a square, homely face. Alone in the Carmel speakroom, Thérèse announced her plan, and Mother Gonzague[13] respectfully explained that the Carmelites did not accept applicants at nine years of age.[14] But the child impressed the prioress. A couple of months later, when Thérèse suffered headaches after Pauline's departure, Mother Gonzague wrote to her, "I learned that my little daughter, Thérèse of the Child Jesus, was not sleeping much and that she is ailing. I'm coming to tell my angelic child that she mustn't be thinking all day long about Agnes of Jesus (Pauline); this would tire out our little heart and could harm our health! . . . I allow my future little daughter to think only of her holy little Carmelite sister in the presence of the Jesus of her heart but never during the night. *Thérèse is to sleep all night, and she is to eat everything her beloved sister Marie wants her to eat.* . . . If my dear little daughter follows what I advise her to do, she will strengthen her health and will be able to come to see her Agnes of Jesus again, and like her, she will become a good and fervent *Spouse of Jesus!* . . . You have a big place in my heart."[15] "Little daughter," "Spouse of Jesus" were phrases used for nuns. "Thérèse of the Child Jesus" is the form a nun's name would take. Mother Gonzague also gave Pauline the permission to write to Thérèse during Lent before her First Communion. Thérèse's decision to seek entry to the Carmel at age 14 only made explicit, and set a very early time for, something that had been in the air since Pauline left home. Louis, too, had sensed that Thérèse might want to enter the Carmel.[16] But there is a world of difference between a child's dreaming of marriage and announcing the day. After she told her sisters at Carmel, Thérèse had to face Louis.

Only four weeks before Thérèse approached him, Louis had suffered a slight stroke that affected his left side. Little by little he was losing what he held dear in life. First Zélie, then Pauline, and only six months before Thérèse came to him, Marie. Marie's decision stunned him — she didn't seem the type for the cloister. "Ah! . . . ah!" he gasped the day she told him, "but . . . without you!"[17] Quickly Louis checked his own emotions and blessed Marie's choice of a life as he had Pauline's. And as the summer approached, Léonie, the troubled daughter, planned once again to enter a convent.

When Thérèse told Louis she wanted to enter the Carmel before Christmas he was sitting in the garden on a

Sunday afternoon in May. She cried, and Louis broke down too. In a weakened state, facing now the loss of his youngest, the 63-year-old Louis did a very tender thing, which reveals how sentimentally he thought of Thérèse. "Going up to a low wall, he pointed to some *little white flowers*, like lilies in miniature, and plucking one of them, he gave it to me, explaining the care with which God brought it into being and preserved it to that very day. While I listened I believed I was hearing my own story . . . in gathering it, Papa had pulled all its *roots* out without breaking them." To Thérèse the flower seemed a symbol of herself, "destined to live on in another soil."[18] In the bittersweet emotions of that May afternoon Thérèse thought her life was settled. Her father had blessed her plans to enter Carmel. From her romantic perch upon the world nothing, it seemed, stood in her way.

The newspapers were filled that spring and summer with the story of the brutal slaughter of two women and an 11-year-old child. In July Henri Pranzini was condemned to death for the crime. *La Croix*, a right-wing newspaper that headlined the sensational, reported every grisly detail of the murders. To the outraged public, Pranzini became the essence of passion, brutality, nihilism, all of which threatened the traditional way of life of decent French people.[19] Thérèse, who believed prayer could save "sinners," decided to test this belief by praying for Pranzini — not just an occasional prayer, but an all-out effort. Despite her father's rule against reading newspapers, she followed the story, with only Céline sharing her secret.

Throughout July and August Thérèse prayed and searched the newspaper accounts for a definite sign that her prayers were effective. Pranzini showed no remorse. The 30th of August he was executed by the guillotine.[20] The next day Thérèse hungrily read the account in *La Croix* and learned that at the moment when he was to place his neck on the guillotine Pranzini had grabbed a crucifix and kissed it three times. Thérèse was ecstatic.

This, she believed, was the sign that her prayers had saved the murderer's soul.[21]

With the fall approaching, Louis Martin planned another pilgrimage — this one in November to Rome, and this time he would take Céline and Thérèse. But first Thérèse had to face a bit of unfinished, and perhaps unpleasant, business. In all this time she had not yet faced her Uncle Isidore to ask for his permission to enter the Carmel, and Isidore Guérin took quite seriously his role as deputy guardian of the Martin girls. He had blessed Pauline and Marie when they chose to leave home, but Pauline had been 21, Marie 26 and both stable young women. Isidore considered Thérèse a coddled child, an indulged child, oversensitive and undereducated. He was a conservative Catholic who believed in the validity of a vocation to religious life and also in the values of middle-class European society — health, education, a comfortable home, art lessons for the children, vacations by the sea. How could he sanction the wish of a 14-year-old girl with a history of emotional instability to confine herself to a cloister?

Thérèse put off the chore of asking her uncle's permission until a Saturday morning in October, a busy day at the Guérin pharmacy.[22] He listened, lowered his book, and gave what she termed "a *very* AFFECTIONATE little sermon."[23] Actually the sermon was not so little — Isidore was a man of words, though in this case only one word counted — no. "He forbade me to speak about my vocation to him until I was seventeen. It was contrary to human prudence, he said, to have a child of fifteen enter Carmel. This Carmelite life was, in the eyes of many, a life of mature reflection, and it would be doing a great wrong to the religious life to allow an inexperienced child to embrace it. . . . I saw all reasoning with him was useless and so I left."[24] Though Isidore still intimidated Thérèse, since the days when he thundered "Blue Beard" with her on his lap she had learned to doubt her uncle's judgment — especially about herself. Woven through his concern for her she discerned a motive far less pure. "It is only the world, I believe, which is the obstacle," Thérèse wrote to Pauline. "It would be a real *public scandal* to see a child entering Carmel; I would be the only one in all of France, etc."[25] Public reaction may well have bothered Isidore, but if Thérèse doubted his motives, he also doubted hers. It was not unlikely that Thérèse, still wounded by the loss of her second mother, was simply following Pauline. Pauline now faced the question of whether her uncle or Thérèse were being unreasonable. After two weeks of worrying, praying and observing Thérèse "so pale, so sad, so unhappy," Pauline wrote Isidore an impassioned letter.

> A thousand thoughts, more *human* than divine come to my mind, especially this bitter reflection which would condemn both Sister Marie . . . and myself: It is her sisters who have attracted her! . . . And this other reflection: What a Father! He does not love His Children, He wants to get rid of them, that's evident.
>
> But Jesus, in his turn, scolded His lamb. He reproached her for her small spirit of faith. . . . "Am I not the Master of hearts? Which is better, to listen to My voice or that of the blind and senseless world? . . . I will be stronger than all of you. I want this child. She is a lily bud opened before the dawn. She is a fruit ripened before the autumn. From on high, I have desired this lily, the beauty of this fruit. . . . My divine hand is ready to pluck My treasure. . . . Who will dare say to Me: Lord, it is too soon, if I find that it is time? . . ."[26]

Apparently Isidore Guérin was moved by this plea from his favorite niece. He withdrew his objection the day after he received Pauline's letter.[27]

The next day, a Sunday, Thérèse rushed to the Carmel to tell Pauline the news and learned that the battle had just begun. No one had considered another man in Lisieux who held authority in this matter over both Thérèse and the prioress of the Carmel, and who also took a dim view of 15-year-old girls joining the cloister — Canon Delatroëtte, the pastor of St. Jacques Church and the ecclesiastical superior of the Carmel. Canon Delatroëtte refused to listen to a request from Thérèse to enter the cloister before she was 21. With the minimum age for entrance set at 16 by the constitution of the order, the canon was stricter than the Rule, and the Rule offered Thérèse no help. She had to have a dispensation.

The game would seem to have been played out, but getting what she wanted was as natural to Thérèse as food. She did not stop with priests. When the Abbé Domin passed over her for the honor of reciting a public prayer on First Communion day, choosing his niece instead — Thérèse wept and carried on at home until the family feared a relapse of her illness. She had her way. Madame Guérin, Marie, Céline and Thérèse went to the Abbé Domin to ask him to choose Thérèse instead of his niece — which he did.[28]

The very Sunday that she heard the canon's decision, Thérèse and Louis appeared at the door of St. Jacques' rectory. Canon Delatroëtte, a man in his seventies, sharp-featured with thick eyebrows, greeted the Martins "coldly." It was a stiff visit as the three sat in the rectory parlor on that rainy Sunday afternoon. The canon told Thérèse that if being a Carmelite meant so much to her she could lead the life at home, but she would not receive his permission to enter until she was 21. She was free to appeal to the bishop, if she wished, but this was his final word. Outside in the rain Thérèse sobbed in fury at the canon's ruling. She would, she cried, petition the bishop, and if he refused, the pope! And Louis consoled her, and nodded, and agreed softly to whatever she wished.[29] But their pilgrimage was scheduled to leave Paris for Rome in two weeks, a very short time to squeeze in a trip to Bayeaux and an appointment with the bishop, even for someone as strong-willed as Thérèse.

It poured down rain again the day that Thérèse and Louis arrived in Bayeaux. Soaked through, the pair rode a bus to the cathedral to dry off before their audience with the bishop. As they slipped past the heavy door into the back of the church they saw that a funeral was in progress — priests crowded the altar and the pews were filled with the ladies of Bayeaux in somber mourning clothes.

As was his custom, Louis headed up the aisle to the front, and His Excellency Bishop Hugonin may have had his first glimpse of Thérèse Martin trotting behind her father, her hat and bright dress dripping water on the stone floor.[30]

The bishop's vicar general, Abbé Révérony, a friendly man in his fifties with short-cropped hair and eyes set close together, led Thérèse and Louis through the halls and formal rooms of the bishop's huge residence. Though Thérèse had tried to look older by piling her hair on top of her head, as she followed the two men through the large still rooms with pictures of bishops staring down from the walls she felt, she said, like an ant.[31]

Bishop Hugonin was a warm, stout man with a sense of humor and long hair that curled just below his ears. He had a placid, square face with eyes set wide apart, and as he listened to this 14-year-old child ask to enter a convent he thought of her father. She might stay just a little longer at home, he suggested. Then it was Louis' turn to speak up and defend Thérèse. He told the bishop just how determined she was — if His Excellency refused her request she was going to the pope. Now as the three sat in their huge armchairs by the fire the bishop uttered the fatal words. Before making his decision he must consult, he said, the ecclesiastical superior of the Carmel of Lisieux, Canon Delatroëtte. Thérèse broke down and cried in the bishop's arms. the attempts at formality and impressions past, Louis told the bishop about Thérèse's grown-up hairdo as they walked to the garden, and he loved the story.[32]

Abbé Révérony had witnessed the whole scene. Since he would lead their section of the pilgrimage to Rome the following week, the Martins chatted with him before leaving. the priest was more impressed by Louis than Thérèse, for he had seen zealous young girls before, not infrequently accompanied by reluctant, if not resistent, fathers. Here was an aging man with three daughters gone, pressing to let his youngest enter a convent. As they discussed the proper dress for the papal audience, Louis asked Abbé Révérony, "Am I good enough as I am?"[33]

The following Friday Thérèse, Céline and their father rose in the middle of the night and slipped through the dark town of Lisieux past the sleeping Carmel to board the 3:00 a.m. train for Paris. In the next two days Thérèse, who had traveled nowhere before but to Alençon and the sea, whirled through the sights of Paris — the Louvre, the Bastille, the Champs-Elysées, the grand opera, the circus, "a beautiful exhibition of machines for making beer."[34] On Sunday an exhausted Thérèse wrote to her sisters in Lisieux, "Everything is turning around me. Tomorrow we shall no longer be in France. I cannot get over all I am seeing . . . Céline is going to tell you if she wants the marvels of Paris; as for myself, I'll tell you only that I am thinking *very often* of you. The beautiful things of Paris don't captivate my heart in the least."[35]

What did captivate her young heart was the romance of martyrdom. Like many a French Catholic girl who read the story of Joan of Arc, Thérèse dreamed that she, too, was "born for *glory*,"[36] and the place most thoroughly soaked with the blood of early Christian martyrs was, of course, the Colosseum in Rome. "I was finally gazing upon that arena where so many martyrs had shed their blood. . . . I was already preparing to kneel down and kiss the soil they had made holy, but what a disappointment!

The place was nothing but a heap of ruins, and the pilgrims were expected to be satisfied with simply looking at these. A barrier prevented them from entering the ruins. No one would be tempted to do so. But was it possible to come all the way to Rome and not go down into the Colosseum? For me it was impossible! . . . One thought raced through my mind; get down into the arena!"[37] When she saw her chance Thérèse, followed by Céline, darted off while the guide was pointing out *"the little CORNICES carrying figures of CUPIDS*; and so neither he nor the *priests* knew anything about the joy that inundated our hearts." Down in the arena the girls kissed "the dust stained with the blood of the first Christians."[38]

The tour also visited an Italian Carmelite monastery where for centuries the monks had maintained the tradition of a cloister strictly forbidden to women. Thérèse slipped inside the cloister when "all of a sudden I saw a good old Carmelite friar at a little distance making a sign for me to leave. But instead of going I approached him and, showing him the cloister paintings, I made a sign that they were beautiful. He undoubtedly understood by the way I wore my hair and from my youthful appearance that I was only a child, so he smiled at me kindly and left. He saw he was not in the presence of an enemy."[39] It was her first encounter with the Italian Church's strict attitude toward women. "I still cannot understand," she wrote years later, 'why women are so easily excommunicated in Italy, for every minute someone was saying, 'Don't enter here! Don't enter there, you will be excommunicated!' Ah! poor women, how they are misunderstood! . . . In heaven He will show that His thoughts are not men's thoughts, for then the *last will be first*. More than once during the trip I hadn't the patience to await heaven to be first."[40]

The climax of the trip was the audience with His Holiness, Pope Leo XIII. As she prepared for the pilgrimage Thérèse had a single thought in mind — to take this chance to speak to the pope about entering the Carmel. If "the Holy Father," who would surely be able to read her soul, said yes, the canon and the bishop must agree. As the moment neared, the nuns back in the Carmel became more tightly linked with Thérèse in her determination. At times nearly daily letters passed between the pilgrims and the nuns back home, with Pauline finally writing emphatically that Thérèse must speak to the pope. "Pay no attention to the crowd which will be around you. What does it matter if they hear you? *Not the least bit.*" And not only Mother Gonzague but also Mother Geneviève, the foundress of the Lisieux Carmel, agreed. Speak up, Pauline coached, even if he passes by, speak up to the pope, but "let M. Révérony know nothing about this letter."[41] As the day of the papal audience drew near, one thought blanched out the sights of Rome — "I had to *dare* to *speak to the Pope* in front of everybody," Thérèse wrote. "This thought made me tremble."[42]

On the appointed Sunday the Martins dressed according to instructions. "The style of dress for the pontifical audience is as follows: for men, a black suit, tie and white or black vest, no gloves. . . . Women should be in black silk or woolen dresses, a black veil covering the head, no gloves."[43] Thérèse first glimpsed Pope Leo XIII at the Mass. Afterward she and Céline took their places at the end of a long line of darkly clad pilgrims which slowly inched its way toward the papal chair. Thérèse described the scene:

> Leo XIII was seated on a large armchair; he was dressed simply in a white cassock, with a cape of the same color, and on his head was a little skullcap. Around him were cardinals, archbishops, and bishops, but I saw them only in general, being occupied solely with the Holy Father. We passed in front of him in procession; each pilgrim knelt in turn, kissed the foot and hand of Leo XIII, (and) received his blessing. . . .[44]

Standing next to the pope was none other than Abbé Révérony. As Thérèse neared the papal chair Abbé Révérony — who had heard Louis Martin tell Bishop Hugonin that Thérèse intended to take her case to the pope — announced that no one was to speak to the Holy Father.[45]

As Thérèse knelt in front of the pope and kissed his foot he stretched out his hand for her to kiss his ring as everyone in the long line had done. But Thérèse did not kiss the ring. She grabbed his knees and blurted out her much rehearsed question: "Most Holy Father, I have a great favor to ask of you . . . Holy Father in honor of your Jubilee permit me to enter Carmel at the age of 15!"[46] There was silence, an embarrassed pause, for Pope Leo XIII at the age of 77 was nearly deaf. Since he couldn't make out what this young girl was saying he turned to Father Révérony to find out. "Most Holy Father, this is *a child*," Thérèse heard him say, "who wants to enter Carmel at the age of fifteen, but the Superiors are considering the matter at the moment."[47]

Now Pope Leo spoke to Thérèse, but not the words she wanted to hear. "Well, my child, do what the superiors tell you!" he said. With nothing rehearsed beyond the simple words of her request, still kneeling, Thérèse leaned her hands right on the pope's knees and said, "Oh Holy Father if you say yes, everybody will agree!" The pope, Thérèse reported, "gazed at me steadily, and he said 'Go . . . go . . . *you will enter if God wills it.*" Still she knelt, immobilized, as if some magnet held her to the spot of her final hope. She did not go even after a nudge from the Swiss Guards. She did not go at all on her own. The Swiss Guards, helped by Abbé Révérony, picked her up and carried her, sobbing, out the door.[48] "The good Pope is so old," Thérèse wrote back to the Carmel, "that one would say he is dead; I would never have pictured him like this. He can hardly say anything. It is M. Révérony who talks."[49]

Thérèse had seen the pope on Sunday. On the following

Thursday the citizens of Lisieux were treated to an account of the papal audience which appeared in the pages of *L'Univers*. "Among the pilgrims was a young girl of 15 who begged the Holy Father for permission to enter a convent immediately to become a Religious. His Holiness encouraged her to be patient, to pray very much, and to seek counsel from God and her conscience. This caused the young girl to break down into sobs."[50]

That Thérèse had gone over the heads of the local authorities to the pope himself escalated the episode. It seemed a stab at Canon Delatroëtte, and now the old prelate dug in his heels. The night the article appeared in the paper the halls of the Lisieux Carmel resonated with more than bells — they rung with the very unpeaceful voice of the canon. "Never had I seen him before as he was on Thursday," Pauline wrote to Rome. "He said that the more he goes on, the more he is rooted in his *no*, and what a no! If you had only heard him! We can see so well that nothing could change him."[51]

Pauline suspected that the canon's position hardened not because of his principles but because of a still unhealed wound. Another daughter of another prominent local family had wanted to enter the Carmel, and her father, M. Fleuriot, charged the canon with unduly pressuring a young woman into a convent. "This poor father has been so calumniated by Monsieur (Fleuriot) at the time of his daughter's plan. It was frightful. . . . And what would Monsieur (Fleuriot) say today when seeing him giving us a child of fifteen?"[52] As the pressure increased the canon became more rigid. "If your little sister should get sick because of grief," he told Pauline, "I shall say that she did not have the strength to be a Carmelite. That's it. But this would not make me give in."[53]

Another priest turned up at the Carmel after the local report of Thérèse's visit to the pope — Father Lepelletier, the young priest who had listened to Thérèse's confession for the past year and a half. He was plainly baffled —

Thérèse Martin begging the pope to enter a convent! It seems that in all that time Thérèse had never even mentioned her plans to her confessor. Unlike Canon Delatroëtte, Father Lepelletier's judgment was unaffected by hurt pride. "He said," reported Pauline, "this child is privileged and destined for great things."[54]

The priest's words bouyed them up, but did not help the case. With all the appeals exhausted now, the pope silent, the final word lay with the bishop. The lines tightened, the intrigue shifted further underground. The plan, spelled out back at the Carmel, was for Thérèse to win over Abbé Révérony. "Everything must come from Monseigneur and you," Pauline wrote to Céline, "and nothing must give rise to the suspicion that the Carmel is acting in an underhanded way."[55] The strategists underrated their key ally — Louis Martin. Three days after the papal visit Louis was visiting a Christian brother in Rome when Abbé Révérony walked in. With disarming simplicity Louis asked Father Révérony about the bishop's decision and told him how upset Thérèse was. "You know very well that you had promised to help me," Louis berated him. Céline reported, "M. Révérony was touched, I believe, and he is beginning to believe that Thérèse's vocation is extraordinary. He even said, 'Well! I will assist at the ceremony; I'm inviting myself.' "[56]

But could Abbé Révérony's word be trusted? After observing the priest's character at close hand for three weeks, Céline thought him a chameleon. "He is always in agreement with everybody; he says one thing with some and another thing with others. What can he be held to?"[57] Thérèse also saw something other than a simple soul. A few days after the papal audience the pilgrimage stopped in the town of Assisi with its Medieval houses of pale pink stone. Thérèse lost a belt in the Church and rummaged through the aisles so long that all but one of the carriages had left — the one remaining was Father Révérony's. Only the most prestigious of nobles had ridden in Father

44

Révérony's coach, and no woman had set foot in it throughout the entire trip. Embarrassed, Thérèse climbed in and took a seat among the gentlemen. "Before we reached the station, all the *great personages* took their huge purses out to give some money to the driver (already paid). I did the same thing, taking out my *very* little purse. Father Révérony did not agree with what I drew out from it, some pretty *little* coins, and instead he offered a *large* coin for both of us."[58] Neither mentioned the burning question.

A couple of days later the pilgrimage was preparing to leave from Nice at 7:00 a.m. while it was still dark. In the confusion of transporting nearly 200 people to the station the Martins were in the same bus with Father Révérony. Before they stepped in Louis whispered to the priest, "Would you say something to Thérèse." Abbé Révérony smiled. With 16 people jammed into the coach, Thérèse was wedged next to the priest.

"Well! where will we go when we are at Lisieux?" he asked her.

"I will go to see my sisters at Carmel."

"We will do what we can, won't we," said Father Révérony.

"Oh, yes!" she said.

"I *promise* to do all I *can*," he said.[59]

The train from Paris to Lisieux carried home a wiser young woman. The lessons of that trip regarding human nature were far more lasting than the sights of Paris. The doctrine of papal infallability had been proclaimed, amidst controversy, only 17 years before the Martins' pilgrimage. In the minds of many simple believers the mantle of the Holy Spirit guarding the pope against teaching error to the Church on matters of faith or morals extended to the man himself. The "Holy Father" was enveloped in a mystique. His name was uttered with the reverence due a saint. For a teenaged Catholic girl no living man seemed closer to God or more able to read the lines of a soul.

Thérèse had seen the reality — a half-deaf, clearly failing old man — yet reacted without a hint of disillusionment. The sight of the very human Pope Leo simply bore out what Thomas à Kempis said — "I found no help at all on earth," she later wrote, "which appeared to me as an arid desert without water. All my hope was in God *alone*. I had just made (sic) the experience that it was much better to have recourse to Him than to His saints."[60]

The trip yielded other revelations. Thérèse ran in the company of the nobility of France and found "all these titles . . . nothing but smoke. From a distance, this had sometimes thrown a little powder in my eyes, but close up, I saw that 'all that glistens is not gold.' "[61] In her opinion her father conveyed more natural dignity than any noble on the trip. But the most lasting impact on her life came not from seeing the nobles' feet of clay, but the priests'.

About 75 priests went on the trip to Rome.[62] In Thérèse's eyes priests were haloed by distance and grace of sacred function. Priests taught religious mysteries in the classroom, heard her confession and forgave her sins, spoke the words of consecration high on the church altar. "To pray for sinners attracted me, but to pray for the souls of priests, whom I believed to be as pure as crystal, seemed puzzling to me! I understood *my vocation* in *Italy* and that's not going too far in search of such useful knowledge. I lived in the company of many *saintly priests* for a month and I learned that, though their dignity raises them above the angels, they are nevertheless weak and fragile men."[63] Weak priests shook her faith no more than did the failing pope. In each case they spoke to her not of the truth of faith, but only of men. They led her to a decision — she would spend her life at Carmel praying, not mainly for "great sinners," but for priests. Thérèse believed in the dogma of redemption — Christ's suffering redeemed other people. She believed she could offer her own life, sufferings, prayers in Carmel to renew the spirit of priests.

It was December when the pilgrims pulled into Lisieux. Feelings, and tension, ran high. The strategists in Carmel made one last effort to move the canon so that Thérèse could join them by Christmas. He came to visit Mother Geneviève, the sweet, elderly foundress of the Lisieux Carmel. Mother Gonzague had persuaded her to use this chance to ask him to admit Thérèse, in front of the entire community. Canon Delatroëtte was enraged. "With all these requests is one to believe that the community's salvation depends on this child's entrance? Let her stay with her father until she is 21."[64] He came back to the Carmel later and accused Mother Gonzague of interfering.[65]

The last hope to obtain approval by Christmas now appeared to be a direct appeal to Bishop Hugonin with Thérèse writing to him herself. Mother Gonzague was skeptical of this approach, Pauline thought they should give up after the canon's explosion, but Thérèse went on and drafted the letter. Even her uncle Isidore was involved now, editing the letter that Thérèse had written. Finally Thérèse mailed her letter to Bishop Hugonin nine days before Christmas. "It is true," she wrote, "that I am very young, but Monseigneur, since God is calling me and Papa is willing!"[66]

With the letter mailed the dust of the battle settled and the vigil began. Each morning of the week before Christmas Louis and Thérèse walked together to Mass, and then along the familiar route down the hill into town to the post office to look for the bishop's reply. Christmas Eve, still the bishop remained silent. Thérèse attended midnight Mass not in the chapel of the Carmel as she had planned, but at St. Pierre Cathedral.

But Father Révérony had kept his word. Three days after Christmas the bishop's answer came to the Carmel — Thérèse could enter without delay. Then in an odd turnabout the prioress withheld the news from Thérèse and Mr. Martin until New Year's Day. In the speakroom the pair learned that Pauline had backed down. She wanted

Thérèse to wait until Easter. According to Marie, Pauline began to worry about Thérèse withstanding the severe Lenten fast, though Pauline claimed later that the decision was to appease Canon Delatroëtte. But the reason mattered little. News of a three-month delay shocked Thérèse, who wept, and Louis, who erupted right there in the Carmel speakroom. ". . . he pointed his finger, saying, 'She (Pauline) is always the same; she says something, then she takes it back.' Oh! he was angry . . . he had gone to so much trouble so that she could enter at Christmas."[67]

Instead of stepping into the place of her dreams, Thérèse walked back up the hill, to the house that seemed empty, to begin three months of waiting.

She had braced for the new life of the Carmel, not the old life at home. "This trial had a particular characteristic about it: I saw all my *bonds broken* as far as the world was concerned."[68] Once again Léonie was back home, as she had been the year before at the same time, from another try at yet another convent. She warned Thérèse that a nun's life was very hard indeed.[69] With three months to wait and Léonie's grim talk of the convent, events threatened to demoralize Thérèse. She decided to begin living "*a serious* and *mortified* life." The word "mortification" was as common in Catholic households as "prayer." To Céline the word meant finding "a thousand ways" to suffer, a not uncommon interpretation in those days. But Thérèse disliked this form of asceticism. "I had no attraction for this. . . . My mortification consisted in breaking my will, always so ready to impose itself on others, in holding back a reply, in rendering little services without any recognition, in not leaning my back against a support when seated."[70] The key phrase for the strong-willed Thérèse was breaking her will.

The final words on Thérèse's entrance to the Carmel came in letters from Abbé Révérony and from Canon Delatroëtte. Father Révérony wrote to Thérèse, "I gladly share in your joy. . . . I am counting on your prayers; I have a pressing need of them."[71] In answer to a letter of Thérèse's, Canon Delatroëtte wrote a prophecy. "I am happy that you are asking God for the grace of being a holy Carmelite. With you, I will pray to Him with my whole heart to make you worthy of being numbered among the true daughters of St. Teresa, but I cannot refrain from regretting that you pressed for your entrance with so much insistence. I fear that later on you and your own sisters will have to regret it."[72]

On Ash Wednesday her father gave her a live lamb as a gift. Thérèse was delighted, but that afternoon, only one day old, the lamb died. "It had been too cold in the wagon where it was born. . . . It was hardly born when it suffered and then died," she wrote to Marie. . . . "You don't realize . . . how much the death of this little animal made me reflect. Oh, yes! On this earth we must attach ourselves to nothing, not even the most innocent things, for they fail you at the moment when you are least expecting it."[73]

Thérèse may have linked the Carmel of Lisieux to a desert, but the name was derived from a mountain, or more exactly, a chain of mountains about 25 miles west of the town of Nazareth which points into the Mediterranean Sea. In ancient times Mount Carmel was dotted with caves and rich in oak, olive, carob and pine trees and lush wild greenery all year round from the moist sea air. On this mountain, according to the Old Testament, the prophet Elijah pitted the power of the living God of Israel against the power of the pagan god Baal. Two bulls were slaughtered. When the first bull was dismembered and placed on a pile of wood, Elijah challenged the 450 prophets of Baal to call on their god to send fire.

The prophets of Baal, as the story goes, "performed their hobbling dance around the altar they had made," while Elijah mocked. "Call louder . . . perhaps he is asleep." The prophets of Baal danced themselves into frenzy, gashing their bodies and invoking the name of their god, but no fire came. Then Elijah dismembered his bull and had it doused three times with water until "the water flowed around the altar and the trench itself was full of water." Elijah stood alone before the agitated and bleeding prophets of Baal and asked the God of Israel very simply to let the pagans know " 'that you, Yahweh, are God and are winning back their hearts.' Then the fire of Yahweh fell and consumed the holocaust and wood and licked up the water in the trench."[1]

Two thousand years after Elijah's holocaust, in the 12th century A.D., a small group of world-weary men from the west sought peace on the slopes of Mount Carmel. There they lived in solitude and contemplated the living God. About 50 years later Albert of Jerusalem wrote down a rule for the hermits "who live near the spring on Mount Carmel."[2] "Since *man's life on earth is a time of trial,*" wrote Albert, *"and all who would live devotedly in Christ must undergo persecution, and the devil your foe is on the prowl like a roaring lion looking for prey to devour, you must use every care to clothe yourselves in God's armor so that you may be ready to withstand the enemy's ambush."*[3] Thus, The Rule, amended later in the century by Pope Innocent IV, sought both to strengthen the monks for the battle with the devil and to protect them against the vagaries and deceits of the self, for in the quiet and loneliness of a cell one might simply turn inward and worship oneself.

"The first thing I require is for you to have a Prior,"[4] wrote Albert. He also required that each monk occupy "a separate cell, situated as the lie of the land you propose to occupy may dictate."[5] There were fast days "unless bodily sickness or feebleness, or some other good reason demand a dispensation from the fast; for necessity overrides every law."[6] No monk was to eat meat nor possess anything of his own — all goods were held in common.[7] The monks were to work to stave off idleness, eat meals together listening to the words of scripture, and keep their "loins . . . girt with chastity."[8] After the last common prayers at night until the next day the monks were to remain in silence. *"Your strength,"* wrote Albert, *"will lie in silence and hope."*[9]

The Carmelites offered no animals in sacrifice to their God. They followed the teachings of Jesus, who had lived in the nearby town of Nazareth. It was a rigid and formalistic devotion to God that Jesus was born into — with hundreds of rules governing eating, washing, entering, leaving, praying. One might live by the rules and be cold to the suffering of a sick outcast. Jesus' own brutal execution ended for His followers the blood offerings of the Old Law. Under the New Law, the monks believed that the living God wanted a sacrifice not of animals, but of the self, as Jesus had done. This little band of men withdrew from the restless life of the towns, the group life of the monasteries, and some of the customs of the Church of Jesus that had sprung up in the 1100 years since His death. They withdrew to the mountain to live the solitary, poor life that Jesus had led, to pray as He had prayed. They asked for a Rule not to punish themselves but to wrest themselves free of the grip of old habits and of the body's strong desires.

Each day the monks united themselves with the re-offering of Christ's body and blood to the Father in the unbloody sacrifice of the Mass. At various hours of the morning, afternoon, evening and during the night they gathered again to extend the prayer of the Mass by reciting or chanting the ancient psalms. The new order of monks spread beyond Mount Carmel, for the New Law of Christ rejected not only the blood sacrifice of animals but also the notion that God dwelt in a particular city or on a particular mountain. In 1254 St. Louis of France brought home six Carmelites after the crusade to live by The Rule near the banks of the Seine.[10]

Over the next 300 years the simple austere life, if not the tradition, was corrupted. A 16th-century Spanish woman from the town of Avila who had withdrawn to a convent to find union with God — for by this time there were Carmelite nuns as well as monks[11] — found instead a lively parlor frequented by the local Spanish nobility and nuns slipping out to visit their family and friends. Despite the noise and distraction, Teresa did cultivate an inner life. Years later she abandoned the clutter of that convent taking with her a handful of women who shared the spirit of the first hermits and sought a simple life of solitude.

Teresa and her companions pledged themselves to the primitive Rule. They ate no meat, they worked, kept silence, prayed the Divine Office, spent hours in solitary prayer, and lived like the poor. Their trademark was the habit of coarse wool, a material both cheap and sturdy, and the shoes of the poor — alpargatas — sandals of natural woven hemp. This same spirit imbued a Spanish Carmelite priest in Teresa's era, John of the Cross, who called his own step-by-step journey to shed the attachments of the world and purify the self in order to be open to union with the living God, *The Ascent of Mount Carmel*. At the heart of the reformed Carmelites was the symbolic climbing of the mountain to find God.

Two Discalced (reformed) Carmelite nuns left Spain to open a house in Paris in 1604, and the order spread quietly for the next 200 years. In the year 1838 a pair of brown-robed Carmelite nuns and three novices stopped to see Teresa of Avila's cloak in Paris before riding through a wet March night in a horse-drawn cart covered only with a piece of canvas. The little party of cold nuns arrived in the town of Lisieux at 4:00 a.m. to spend the next five months in cramped quarters while a priest scouted the town for a suitable home. In keeping with the poverty of the order he bought a house in the damp valley of the Orbiquet River, a spot lacking both the symbolic height of a mountain and the drier air.[12] The five nuns moved into the "modest house" and in time added a chapel, choir, library, kitchen, refectory, cemetery, grounds, cells and a brick cloister. Fifty years later one of the nuns who had ridden the cart into Lisieux asked the priest superior in front of the community that had grown to 26 women[13] to admit one more, Thérèse Martin. The act was both bold and of questionable courtesy since Canon Delatroëtte had dropped by on a feast day to greet the aging Mother Geneviève, revered in the Carmel of Lisieux as "The Foundress."[14]

The 26 nuns in the Lisieux Carmel in 1888 dressed alike

in brown habits and bore saints' names. The external symmetry failed to level the differences in temperament. There was, for example, Sister St.-Pierre, old, crippled, irascible, who summoned her helper in the chapel each evening with a shake of her hourglass.[15] And middle-aged Sister St. Vincent de Paul, who could not abide slow workers and had a gruff manner and a habit of making cutting remarks. She was the sandal maker.[16] And 43-year-old Sister Marie of the Angels, sweet and kind and perfectly at peace no matter what menial task she was given, who excelled at embroidery.[17] At 23 Sister Martha of Jesus was the youngest, orphaned as a child, unstable and with a quick temper, a quick tongue, and abrupt changes of mood.[18] The oldest was 83-year-old Mother Geneviève, warm and kind. The average age was nearly 47.[19] Disharmony was sharpened by the rule of lifelong enclosure — allowing not even a brief change of scene[20] — but muted by the rigid daily schedule.

The nuns rose at 5:00 in the summer and 6:00 in the winter.[21] Silently they removed the linen veils in which they had slept and dressed in woolen underwear, the floorlength brown habit of coarse wool, and cord sandals. Minutes later the cell doors all along the dark hallways opened and the hall was filled with silent dark figures. They filed into the choir and took their places in the oak stalls beneath six pairs of huge wood shutters which arched to a graceful point. The nuns prayed quietly in the shadow of the double grilles cast by the sanctuary lamp.

Then the prioress intoned the first of the hours of the Divine Office, in Latin, recited in monotone on ordinary days, chanted on Sundays and feast days.[22] Later in the day the community would gather again for Vespers, Compline, Matins and Lauds. After the psalms and the readings the Mass began, and on the days permitted by the prioress each nun would kneel in turn in front of a small opening in the grille, just large enough for the priest to place a consecrated host on the waiting tongue.

After Mass the nuns passed single file into the refectory, a large, open, sunny room with wood paneling halfway up the walls, a tiled floor, and heavy wood tables rimming the edge. Each nun would bow before the crucifix and slip into her place, where a crockery bowl, a dish and a pitcher were set, and a knife and wooden spoon laid crosswise on a napkin in front of the bowl. There were no forks — in Teresa of Avila's time forks were not in use. At the signal from the prioress, all would sit and pin a napkin from the shoulders to the table to ensure that not even a crumb would be lost. As they ate a rough, thick, plain meatless soup, they listened to readings from a spiritual book. It was 8:00 a.m. They had been up for three hours.

The first real meal of the day came later in the morning — fish or eggs, never meat, a large portion of vegetables, and cheese or fruit. Portions were scooped onto the plates in advance and under obedience one ate what one was given. After the meal came recreation. In the summer the community gathered outdoors and in the winter they clustered about the wood fire in the recreation room, the only heat in the monastery.[23] Drawn into a circle, baskets of sewing at their feet, the sisters chatted cheerfully in a group. Recreation ended with a bell, and at noon began an hour of silence which might be used to write letters, or in the summertime for a siesta. This was the only free time.

Five hours a day the nuns spent at work, which included cooking, nursing the sick nuns, cleaning, sewing, making the small wafers of unleavened bread for use as hosts, beating the clothes clean in the large square pool of water such as the French villages used for laundry, and in the summer haying in the meadow. In addition to these jobs the nuns spent their afternoons saying the Divine Office and praying privately, and at 6:00 once again filed into the refectory in silence for another meatless soup, another large portion of a vegetable, cheese or fruit, and spiritual reading. After the evening's recitation of the Divine Office the solemn "grand silence" began. In 1888, to avoid rising in the middle of the night, as had the monks on Mount Carmel, the nuns recited Matins and Lauds — the hours normally sung during the night — before they went to bed. After each had reflected on her thoughts and conduct that day, the silent file of nuns flowed back down the corridors and disappeared into the cells. Linen veils were donned for sleep and at 11:00 the oil lamp in each cell went out.

Over the centuries the spirit of Albert's primitive Rule of solitude, fasting, labor and silence bred with voices that stirred fear and guilt and preached fiery judgment, voices that infected the monastery of Lisieux no less than the convent schools. The air at the Carmel was thick with the words offense, reparation, judgment, imperfection, fault. The nuns meditated on a 585-page book called *The Treasure of the Carmel* which contained the rules and traditions of the past — both pure and alloyed. "It is necessary to tremble," wrote one 17th century commentator, "every time we go to the choir to say the office. It is necessary to have a great reserve in the presence of God, for you must know there are no faults that God pardons less than those done in chanting his praises."[24]

Ascetic practices called "mortifications" and "humiliations" had also crept into the monasteries. One such practice at the Lisieux Carmel was for a nun to kneel in the center of the dining hall with her arms outstretched as on a cross. Another was for her to beg for her food.[25] Still another, called simply "the discipline," was practiced on Friday.[26] The discipline was self-flagellation.

Central to The Rule was obedience to the prioress who, in 1888, was Marie Adèle Rosalie Davy de Virville,[27] intelligent, educated, from the noble class, tall, with an unfortunately homely face, but a commanding posture and manner and what everyone agreed was a lovely, resonant voice.She entered the Carmel of Lisieux at the age of 26 the very year that Zélie and Louis Martin's first child was born. In the Carmel Marie Davy de Virville found women

56

less well educated than she, and of a lower class. In addition to her mellifluous voice she was generous, a fine conversationalist, performed "extraordinary penances," possessed a lively sense of humor and "a heart of gold," and had "a passion of jealousy."[26]

One summer day in 1867 she bolted into the garden in what was described by witnesses as "a fit of jealousy." When the nuns found her crouched behind a ladder they led her to the prioress. As she entered the office she darted for the window to fling herself out, a gesture more melodramatic than dangerous, for the window was on the first floor. Because she was already sub-prioress of the Carmel, the incident was hushed up.[29] Seven years later the petulant sub-prioress, whose religious name was Sister Marie de Gonzague, was elected prioress, which office she held, with some interruption, for a total of 21 years.

Like her attempt to throw herself out the window, Mother Gonzague's abuse of office was prosaic. It rose out of impulses and her attachment to her status, her class and her cat. From time to time she asked the novices to search for her pet cat, Mira, when it wandered off in the evening. They had to scout the garden and call the cat even over the monastery wall.[30] While the nuns fasted on meatless soups and vegetables, Mother Gonzague's cat dined on veal liver and sweetened milk. If the cat killed a bird the bird was served to it roasted, with sauce.[31]

When her sister, a countess, needed funds Mother Gonzague could not bear to see her sell off her silver and lace.[32] So she loaned her sister an amount of money in excess of the purchase price of the original house of the Carmel — from the Carmel's coffers. Mother Gonzague failed to keep an exact account of the occasional bank notes she received in repayment.[33] The countess came to treat the Carmel of Lisieux as a second home, the nuns as servants. Though she did not violate the cloister, she and her grandchildren had the run of the superior's parlor and a nearby room when they came to town.[34] The nuns were expected to offer tapestries and napkins embroided by hand for no payment other than the honor of the countess's compliments. During a particularly odious infection, her medical bills and medicine were paid by Mother Gonzague and the cloths used to wrap the infected area were washed by hand by one of the Carmelite nuns.[35]

Such a climate was less than ideal for the life of solitude and silence. Moreover, Mother Gonzague was devoted to the spirit of mortifying the flesh. "Such was the ideal of the Carmel of Lisieux under the government of Mother Marie de Gonzague. Iron crosses and flagellations with nettles held grand honor. In this way they believed they were offering the necessary sacrifices to God."[36]

Over the years the nuns became numb to the prioress's avalanche of trivial suggestions "to see that a certain door was always closed, to refrain from passing by a particular part of the monastery, not to walk *through* the choir."[37] They dreaded, however, the visits of her sister and the disruptions of peace from the periodic "terrible scenes" caused by the prioress's jealousy.[38] Mother Gonzague reigned nearly unchallenged, except for one sister whose education, refinement and power of personality, if not social class, rivaled hers — Pauline Martin.

As the days of Lent 1888 drew to a close, Thérèse prepared to realize her dream. Already disciplining her will at home, she anticipated finding the inner peace Thomas à Kempis spoke of by a life of prayer and by placing herself in unquestioned obedience under the prioress of the Carmel. "It is a great matter to stand in obedience," Thomas said, "to live under a prelate: and not to be our own master."[39] On April 9th the girl who jumped onto the Colosseum floor to touch it for herself rose early to begin her life inside the cloister walls, a place she had never seen.

On the day Thérèse entered the Carmel all the Martins and the Guérins escorted her through the spiked iron gate and heard Mass in the chapel. The nuns were there too, invisible presences behind the grille in the choir which jutted off from the public chapel like the boot of an L. After the communion of the Mass Thérèse "heard nothing . . . but sobs."[40] Inevitably the moment arrived when she must say good-bye to Louis. Unaccustomed to public scenes, conscious of her aunt and uncle and cousins and sisters and the unseen eyes of the nuns, Thérèse knelt formally to ask for her father's blessing. Nothing reveals Louis Martin's natural simplicity and dignity more than his gesture at this moment. When he saw his daughter kneeling in front of him he knelt down with her.[41] In the sacristy they knocked on the metal cloister door, listened as the iron bolts slid back and the huge key grated in the rarely used lock, and the door opened. There stood the prioress, a black veil covering her face.[42] Thérèse passed through the door and it was shut, bolted top and bottom, and relocked with the iron key. The prioress led Thérèse to the darkened choir on the other side of the grille visible in the public chapel. A drape shielded the nuns from view, but since the small communion grate was open they had closed the wood shutters to protect themselves from being seen.[43] Thérèse saw nothing but the darkness. "What struck me first," she said, "were the eyes of . . . Mother Geneviève, which were fixed on me."[44]

Canon Delatroëtte came to the Carmel too the day of Thérèse's entrance. "Well! Reverend Mothers," he said, "you can sing a *Te Deum!* As the delegate of Monseigneur, the Bishop, I present this child of fifteen whose entrance you so desired. I trust she will not disappoint your hopes, but I remind you that if she does, you alone will have to bear the responsibility."[45]

Mother Gonzague herself led Thérèse on a tour of the monastery, out along the walkway lined with chestnut trees, into the meadow, and back through the courtyard rimmed with brick columns and arches and lined on one side with the doors of the nuns' cells. That night Sister

Thérèse of the Child Jesus, as she would be called, followed the line of nuns up the winding stairwell holding a gray metal oil lamp with slits that threw spiked shadows on the word "Silence." She opened the wooden door to her cell and placed the lamp on the shelf in the corner opposite her bed.

The cell was small, about 7' by 10', with stained plaster walls, a bare wood floor, a wood bench, a small writing table for her lap, a large hour glass, a jug of water and a basin on the floor, shuttered windows and a plain wood cross over the bed. There was no heat. The bed was the type found in peasant cottages: wood planks laid across a trestle and covered with a *paillasse* — a canvas bag full of straw. She changed from the dress she still wore — for she would wear her own blue dress and cape and a bonnet for the first few months — and at 11:00 p.m. doused her lamp, slipped in between the wool sheets, pulled up the single blanket of brown wool, and laid her head on a wool-covered pillow.[46] "Everything thrilled me," she wrote later of her first day. "I felt as though I was transported into a desert."[47]

Thérèse was still only 15, and like a normal teenager she craved the approving glance of the prioress. She tried to run into Mother Gonzague in the halls "to find a few crumbs of pleasure."[48] Recognizing herself that delight in another's approval was hardly the point of the life she had pledged to lead, Thérèse resisted her impulse. "I was obliged to walk rapidly by . . . (her) door and to cling firmly to the banister of the staircase in order not to turn back. There came into my mind a crowd of permissions to seek. . . . I found a thousand reasons for pleasing my nature."[49] In fact, the eyes of the prioress were observing Thérèse closely. Her new postulant, the prioress believed, had great potential — provided she was not spoiled. Mother Gonzague set out to ensure that Thérèse did not become the community pet.

Thérèse, innocent of a dust rag, was assigned to work

with Sister Marie of the Angels in the linen room[50] and also to dust and sweep. She was very slow at any sewing, slow in the linen room, and the dusting revived an old fear — Thérèse was afraid of spiders. The sweeping and cleaning took her to the dim alcove beneath the stairs. The gaze of Mother Gonzague extended even to the alcove and one day she found a cobweb. It was the custom at the Carmel to point out "faults" publicly. "We can easily see," said the prioress to the assembled community of nuns, "that our cloisters are swept by a child of fifteen! Go and take that cobweb away and be more careful in the future."[51] For committing a fault Thérèse was required to kneel and kiss the floor. Another of Thérèse's jobs was weeding the garden, which she did at 4:30 in the afternoon, frequently encountering the prioress as she headed outdoors. "Really," snapped Mother Gonzague one day, "This child does nothing at all! What sort of novice has to take a walk every day?"[52]

"Mother Prioress," according to Sister Teresa of Saint Augustine, "was not sparing in her use of reprimands and humiliations where Sister Thérèse was concerned."[53]

Obedience ruled even the meals. Though Thérèse was dispensed from fasting because of her age and served milk and large helpings of the hearty soups and vegetables, the food often did not agree with her. She was obliged to eat everything on her plate.[54] Thérèse said nothing but her stomach rebelled. Sister Marie of the Angels, the novice-mistress, told her to report her stomach aches. As this was an order from a superior Thérèse complied — every day. "I would have preferred to be flogged rather than go and tell her, but out of obedience I did it every time."[55] Sister Marie of the Angels was sweet, sincere, generous and absent-minded.[56] She began sadly murmuring that this poor child would never be quite strong enough for the cloister Rule. When Mother Gonzague heard about Thérèse's daily report of stomach aches, she said: "For goodness sake, that child is always complaining."[57]

The youngest in the community next to Thérèse was 23-year-old Sister Martha of Jesus, also a novice. They got along well despite Sister Martha's sharp tongue and dark moods. Sister Martha, who worked in the kitchen, occasionally served Thérèse leftovers which, according to Marie Martin, were "the most tainted remainders of meals."[58] Thérèse ate whatever was put on her plate. As if the food were not enough to invite indigestion, twice a week Thérèse was expected to ask to perform public "mortifications." On those days she stood in the center of the dining hall with her arms outstretched as the other sisters looked on. "It cost me very much to ask permission to perform acts of mortification in the refectory because I was timid and I blushed," she said a few years later.[59]

But neither the work nor the humiliations, the harshness of the prioress, The Rule, nor the food disillusioned Thérèse. There is no indication that she ever considered returning home as Léonie had done. She maintained that nothing blighted the happiness with which she stepped into the Carmel. "This happiness was not passing. It didn't take its flight with 'the illusions of the first days.' *Illusions*, God gave me the grace not to have *A SINGLE ONE* when entering Carmel. I found the religious life to be *exactly* as I had imagined it."[60]

A familiar sight in Lisieux that spring was Louis Martin making his way down the hill to town with presents tucked under his arm — bottles of wine or a catch of fresh fish. Not that he had the pleasure of handing these to his daughters in person. Carmelites could not accept personal gifts. Louis handed his gifts through a window to a sister who dealt with the outside world and she placed them on a huge rotating wooden shelf, the turnstyle, to be removed on the other side of the wall by anonymous hands.[61] The task of thanking him in the name of the community was assigned to Thérèse:

"They just showed me this instant the birds. Oh! . . . Father, how good you are."[62]

"Your beautiful little candles pleased me so much that I cannot refrain from writing you a little note to thank you."[63]

"How good you are . . . to your little Queen; almost no day passes that she does not receive some present. . . . I kiss you from a distance with my whole heart."[64] In her notes to her father Thérèse was once again the delighted child opening her Christmas shoes.

Louis certainly knew nothing of Thérèse's difficulties, nor is it likely that the Guérins suspected. A month after Thérèse entered the Carmel Mother Gonzague wrote to Madame Guérin that Thérèse was "perfect; never would I have believed in a judgment so advanced in a fifteen-year-old! . . . Not a word has to be said to her; everything is perfect."[65] When the Guérins visited, all three Martin girls came to the speakroom together and Thérèse let Marie and Pauline do the talking. Jeanne Guérin later described a typical visit: "I saw Thérèse only in the convent parlor. . . . Or rather I should say that I guessed she was present, for I neither saw nor heard her. The inflexible Rule condemned me to sit in the parlor in front of a completely closed grille, and I could hardly ever hear (her), . . . because she completely effaced herself to let her sisters do the talking, and said very little herself."[66] Thérèse's silence fit the Guérins view of her. They thought, according to Céline, that "having entered religion too young . . . Thérèse's education had been *tronquee* and she would suffer the effects of this all her life."[67]

But Céline did hear the details of Thérèse's early days in the Carmel. "Pauline especially spoke to me of her annoyance at seeing our little sister badly cared for, exposed to the opposition of several of the nuns, and scolded right and left. On such occasions Thérèse comforted her and assured her that she was happy and had quite enough to live on . . . several times she had nothing on her plate but some herring heads or other rubbish reheated several days in a row."[68]

Between Thérèse and Pauline now stood the Rule. Conversation during recreation was in common, never personal. Private confidence was restricted to spiritual matters with her superiors. The novice-mistress, Sister Marie of the Angels, was a nun formed in the old tradition — very sweet, but lacking the capacity to understand Thérèse. "Her kindness towards me was limitless," Thérèse said later, "and still my soul did not expand under her direction."[69] As for the prioress, "I was unable to meet her without having to kiss the floor, and it was the same thing on those rare occasions when she gave me spiritual direction."[70]

Thérèse had no choice now of a confessor. He was the chaplain to the Carmel, Father Youf, a man described as "austere."[71] He had once told Sister Teresa of Augustine after a confession, "My poor child, all I can tell you is that you already have one foot in hell and that, if you continue, you will soon put the second one there."[72] It is not clear exactly when Thérèse confessed to Father Youf that she was so tired that she sometimes fell asleep during the Mass, but his answer was characteristic. According to Pauline, "He gave her a severe reprimand and told her she was offending God."[73]

Besides the limits of the personalities around her and the restrictions of the Rule, another obstacle prevented Thérèse from freely discussing her difficulties — herself. "It was only with great effort that I was able to take direction, for I had never become accustomed to speaking about my soul and I didn't know how to express what was going on within it."[74] This was the problem when Father Pichon, the priest who had pulled Marie Martin out of the pit of scruples several years before, came to the Carmel at the end of May for Marie's profession. Thérèse liked Father Pichon. He was a warm man with a soft round face and a light touch of humor who affectionately adopted a family nickname for Thérèse — the Benjamin.[75] Before the trip to Rome Thérèse had timidly written to him to ask him to be her personal spiritual director.[76] Now, seven weeks after she began the Carmelite life, the 15-year-old Thérèse sat with the 45-year-old priest whom her family revered — and was unable to talk freely with him. "My interview with the good Father was a great consolation to me, but it was veiled in tears because I experienced much difficulty in confiding in him."[77]

But Father Pichon arrived at a fragile time for Thérèse and relieved her growing anxiety that she was "offending" God. Thérèse made a general confession to him covering her entire life. The emphasis with which she later quoted his statement to her at the end of her confession suggests the power his words had for her: *"In the presence of God, the Blessed Virgin, and all the Saints, I DECLARE THAT YOU HAVE NEVER COMMITTED A MORTAL SIN."*[78] But for all his good will Father Pichon, like her uncle Isidore, did not perceive Thérèse's intelligence. And like Mother Gonzague and Canon Delatroëtte who persisted in calling her "the child," he tended to patronize Thérèse.[79] He told her her "fervor was childish, and . . . (her) way was very sweet," and told her to "thank God for what He has done for you; had He abandoned you, instead of being a little angel, you would have become a little demon."[80] Though he wrote to her occasionally Thérèse never saw Father Pichon again.[81]

On Friday the 15th of June, only two months after Thérèse had left home, Louis Martin sat quietly at his workbench. Céline came in to show him a painting she had just finished and Louis liked the painting so well he proposed that she study art in Paris. Céline's response took her father by surprise. "I immediately answered that I would prefer to give up this art completely rather than expose my soul to any danger."[82] She, too, planned to enter the Carmel. A week later, telling no one, Louis abruptly left home with the intention of living the solitary life of a hermit.[83] On Monday, two days after he had disappeared, Céline received a note from her father from Le Havre asking for money to be sent, but giving no residence address. Céline and Isidore Guérin and a relative of the Guérins went to Le Havre to watch the post office. On Wednesday they found Louis and brought him home.[84]

Helpless at the Carmel, Thérèse received blunt letters from a lonely, frightened Céline. "He appears so old to me now," Céline wrote in July, "so worn out. If you were to see him kneeling every morning at the Communion Table; he leans over, he helps himself as well as he can, and it's enough to make you weep. My heart is torn; I imagine that he will die soon. . . . I am always seeing him in his hour of agony, and my soul is so heavy that I can no longer breathe."[85] Mother Gonzague personally handed Céline's letter to Thérèse after morning prayer[86] before the monastery was fully light. "You know Sunday is sometimes sad," wrote Céline. "I feel emptiness everywhere. . . . Do you remember the evenings in the belvedere, our long chats, our dreams of sanctity? . . . Everything in the house is filled with memories of you. In the little study, the two drawers of your desk have remained intact; if you only knew what heartaches I get when I open them. Everything is arranged as you placed it, your copybooks, your books. . . . In my bedroom, your linen drawer has not been touched. . . . I'm crying while writing these lines."[87]

Thérèse's answer to Céline the next day contrasts remarkably with the tortured tone of Céline's letter. "Yes, life is painful for us," Thérèse wrote her older sister. ". . . Let us raise ourselves above what is passing away . . . let us keep ourselves a distance from the earth. . . . There remains nothing else for us to do but to fight . . . let us lay the axe to the root of the tree. . . . Jesus is asking *ALL, ALL, ALL*."[88] The following week Thérèse wrote to her father in the carefree voice of the "little Queen." "If you only knew the pleasure your carp, your *monster* gave us. The dinner was held back for half an hour. Marie . . .

made the sauce, and it was delicious. . . . It was even better than the sumptuous 'cuisine d'Italie' and that is not saying a little, for what banquets . . . and what company! Do you remember . . . Father?"[89] The lighthearted notes to her father conceal perfectly Thérèse's real views about attaching herself to anything. In September she wrote to thank him for "an avalanche of pears, onions, prunes and apples, which came from the turntable . . . they had less trouble entering than your Queen, who was obliged to go to Rome to have the door opened to her. . . . The enormous onions delighted my heart."[90] A few weeks later Thérèse wrote to Céline "that we should not attach ourselves to what is around us since we could be in another place other than where we are; our affections and our desires would not be the same. I can't explain my thought to you . . . but when I see you I will tell you about it."[91]

The first landmark of Thérèse's religious life was approaching — her robing in the brown wool habit of the order. The ceremony known as the "Taking of the Habit" is elaborate, solemn and, part of it, very public. Louis had sent some Alençon lace for her dress.[92] The day of the taking of the Habit would be the last time in Thérèse's life that she could step out of the cloister and physically embrace her father. But on October 31st Louis suffered another stroke, with paralysis.[93] "Oh! how much I pity Papa!" wrote Céline. "I can see that he is suffering VERY MUCH. Today his poor face had a deathly pallor on it."[94] The superiors considered going ahead with the ceremony without Thérèse leaving the cloister, but finally simply delayed it, a blow to Thérèse. Her disappointment evoked from Mother Gonzague not criticism, but a very motherly reaction. "I don't want the child of my tenderness to allow herself to go into such a great sorrow. . . . I am carrying you in my heart, which blesses you, very darling child!!!"[95] In December Louis improved enough that the ceremony was set for January. As the year of 1888 ended, Thérèse wrote a playful New Year's greeting to her father: "If the guide at Rome were here, he would be able to say '*Messieurs les Abbés*, I am going to have you look upon a father, the like of whom you've never seen; there is something here that will make you fall over in *admiration.*' "[96]

Following custom, the Sunday before the ceremony, which was to take place on Wednesday, January 9th, Thérèse withdrew from the regular routine of the Carmel for a three-day retreat to pray and reflect. During the retreat Thérèse was permitted to speak only with the novice-mistress and the prioress, but she was free to write notes — and write notes she did, a stream of words scribbled on little scraps of paper addressed to Marie and Pauline.[97] Her retreat was filled, not with serenity, but "pinpricks." "Aridity! . . . Sleep! . . . But at least there is silence! . . . Silence does good to the soul. . . . But creatures! Oh! creatures! . . . Those who surround me are very good, but there is something, I don't know what, that repels me! . . . If you only knew how much I want to be indifferent to the things of this earth."[98]

The next day the bishop sent word to the Carmel that because of a funeral Thérèse's ceremony had to be delayed until Thursday.[99] Thérèse had set her heart on the 9th, the anniverary of her entrance to Carmel. She wrote to Pauline the now familiar lesson, Jesus would not "allow me to attach myself to ANY created thing. He knows well that if He were to give me a *shadow* of HAPPINESS, I would attach myself to it with all my energy, all the strength of my heart, and this shadow He is refusing me; He prefers leaving me in darkness to giving me a false light which would not be *Himself*! . . . Since I can't find *any* creature that contents me, I want to give all to Jesus, and I don't want to give to the creature even one *atom* of my love. . . . Today, more than yesterday, if that were possible, I was deprived of all consolation."[100] "Apparently her sandal-fitting with gruff Sister St. Vincent de Paul had also gone badly. "This morning," Thérèse wrote

Pauline, "I had trouble with Sister St. Vincent de Paul; I went away with a heavy heart."[101] Meanwhile Louis Martin was filling the turnstyle with gifts for the celebration. On Tuesday Thérèse wrote Pauline that she was "immersed in darkness"[102] and the same day wrote to her father, "if you only know how I was touched by your kindness! . . . a melon! . . . champagne!"[103] Wednesday night it rained and was unseasonably warm, with no trace of the snow that Thérèse hoped for.[104] And Pauline, like the mother of the bride, fretted that her father might break down and cry during the ceremony.[105]

But the gloom had lifted the next day as Thérèse, in white velvet and lace, her blond hair falling in loose curls down her back, her head ringed with a crown of lilies, was led out of the cloister by a procession of nuns holding candles. Once outside, Thérèse took Louis' arm and he led her into the chapel as if he were giving away the bride. After the Mass Thérèse reentered the cloister to exchange her bridal clothes for the brown habit, the brown scapular (a long panel of brown wool falling in front and in back), a short white veil over her head — the veil of the novice, the black leather cincture symbolizing servitude, the cord sandals, and a long white cape. A powerful symbol of the ceremony is the cutting of the novice's hair, out of view, while the nuns chant an Israeli psalm of exile. But in yet another reminder of Thérèse's age, another reservation about her ability to endure, the nuns, at that point, did not cut Thérèse's hair.[106]

Thérèse listened as the celebrant reminded her of the austerity of The Rule, the harshness of the life, the solitude. She prostrated herself on the floor, the body-length white cape flaring out to the sides like a fallen eagle. At the close of the ceremony Bishop Hugonin made a happy mistake. Instead of the hymn normally sung that day, he intoned the Te Deum — the great hymn of thanksgiving reserved for the Profession, the day of lifelong vows.[107] And Louis did not break down as he held Thérèse for the last time. Thérèse thought him "so handsome, so *dignified*." The day was unmarred even by the weather. "Nothing was missing," wrote Thérèse, "not even the snow! . . . the monastery garden was white like me!"[108] Her reaction may seem a bit exuberant for one who ended that day in the somber robes of the Carmelite nun. But her bridal ceremony took place only one week after her 16th birthday.

When she embraced her father at the ceremony, Thérèse didn't know how final a parting it was. A month later Louis' mental illness took a sad turn. The mild man who had spent his childhood in military camps began to hallucinate. According to Céline, Louis felt himself immersed in slaughter, battles; he was hearing the sounds of cannon and the drum."[109] To protect the women of his household Louis took up his revolver.[110] Isidore Guérin considered a gun in the hands of an hallucinating man a threat. His method of controlling the situation was to call in a strong friend to forceably disarm Louis. "Léonie and I were mute," wrote a stunned Céline, "we kept silent the whole time; we were crushed, broken."[111] Without telling the confused Louis, Isidore arranged to have him committed to a mental institution — that same day.[112] On the way to the train Louis, docile and unaware that his sudden trip to Caen would end in an institution with 500 inmates, stopped off at the Carmel. Only Pauline was called to the speakroom. "It is I, Pauline," he said, "and I've brought you some fish." Pauline saw "two or three little fish in his handkerchief."[113]

"He is incredibly good," Céline wrote a family friend six days later from Caen,

> he was far from wanting to do us any harm with his revolver; on the contrary, he wanted to defend us . . . he was seeing frightful things. . . . An attempt at robbery in the town served only to confirm him in his ideas, so he took his revolver

and wanted to carry it on him in case of danger, for, he said, "I would not want to harm even a cat." In fact, I don't believe that he would have made use of it; it was just an idea that was passing and it would have vanished. Perhaps they should have waited before acting and should have tried ways of taking it away from him, for he was so good, so gentle. . . .[114]

Isidore Guérin had not waited. Once again he made a quick and fateful decision for the Martin family.

"I recall," Thérèse wrote a few years later, "that in the month of June, 1888 . . . I said: 'I am suffering very much, but I feel I can still bear greater trials. . . .' I didn't know that on February 12 . . . Father would drink the *most bitter* and *most humiliating* of all chalices . . . that day, I didn't say I was able to suffer more!"[115] Thérèse had to face not only the pain of her father's condition and exile, but insinuations and conjectures about the root of what was assumed to be mental illness. Céline, who went to Caen to be near Louis, wrote back to reassure her sisters. "Sister Costard, after having talked about other patients, told me, when speaking about Papa: 'This is not Mr Martin's case, *he is paralyzed.*' She claims that it is rapidly approaching a general paralysis; she finds his tongue a little impaired, his movements are slow, and he walks with difficulty."[116]

Despite the diagnosis of paralysis, Louis was confined in a large dismal mental institution. It seems that in an era ignorant of clinical tests for veneral disease, mental symptoms such as Louis displayed in a man his age evoked the suspicion of syphilis.[117] And the people of Lisieux had their own interpretation, whispered about the town until it seeped through the walls of the Carmel. Poor Mr. Martin, it was said, was driven out of his wits by the loss of his daughters, especially the youngest.[118]

A few weeks after the episode with the revolver,

71

Céline, still in Caen, wrote a breathless letter to Thérèse.

If you only knew what I dreamt the other night! You had just died a martyr: a man had taken you into the woods to kill you. With envy I saw you leave for martyrdom. . . . I was awaiting what was going to happen when suddenly we saw a light smoke arising to heaven, and then a bird sang. We said to ourselves: the sacrifice is accomplished! Thérèse is a martyr. . . . My heart leaped at the news. And what about me! . . . As I was wandering in the countryside a little boy . . . plunged his awl . . . into my throat . . . the child being undoubtedly too weak, I did not die. . . . He ended up by tearing out my eyes. This time I collapsed but saying always: more, more! . . . I wanted more, but I didn't end up dying; I was envying your lot when . . . I awakened. . . .[119]

If the romance and glory of suffering had ever infatuated Thérèse the appeal was now dead. She wrote to her older sister a gentle but clear reproof. "Céline's dream is very pretty, and perhaps one day it will be carried out . . . but, in the meanwhile, let us begin our martyrdom, let Jesus *tear* from us all that is most dear to us. . . . Before dying by the sword, let us die by pinpricks."[120] Thérèse's belief was being distilled steadily down to one simple notion, not great emotions, great lights, the glory of a public martyrdom or the pious phrases that filled her childhood. "Céline . . . if you only knew my misery. . . . Sanctity does not consist in saying beautiful things, it does not even consist in thinking them, in feeling them! . . . It consists in *suffering*, and suffering *everything*."[121]

Because of the crisis the Carmelite Rule was relaxed. Marie and Pauline were permitted to skip community services and recreation to talk. As the mental institution was a *fait accompli*, their talk was less necessity than outlet for their distress. Thérèse chose not to join them. If the Rule she believed in and the detachment she sought meant anything, it must be lived now. According to one of the nuns, not an admirer of the Martin family, during those leaden days Thérèse "attended the community acts punctually, even when her sisters were discussing family matters. I saw her at recreation, then, when her sisters were absent, and she spoke with us perfectly calmly though the big tears in her eyes showed us that she was not indeed unmoved by these sufferings."[122] Most certainly Thérèse was not unmoved — the strain appeared in her handwriting. The editors of Thérèse's letters indicate that those written between January and May reveal a change: ". . . the irregular and painful motion would cause one to believe in the imminence of an emotional breakdown."[123]

The arena was narrowing with no room for heroic deeds. Thérèse's battle was within herself, fought in a tight space amidst the trivial failures and frustrations that whittle away at the spirit. Assigned to assist Pauline in the refectory, she swept, mended tablecloths (Pauline sometimes scolding her for slowness) and set out pitchers of water and beer.[124] At last Thérèse was close to Pauline, with no chance to pour out her pain. She wore a large iron cross under her habit — for three weeks. The cross was so heavy that it made her sick and she knew that such ascetic practices were not for her.[125] This was also Thérèse's first winter spent in the damp, unheated Carmel and she suffered day and night from the cold.[126] Finally she was surrounded by people insensitive to her, but quite turned in on themselves.

Marie Guérin wrote a letter from Paris spilling over with torment — "I am suffering so much that it does me good to pour all my pains into your heart. Paris was not made for healing the scrupulous; I no longer know where to turn my eyes. If I flee from one nudity, I meet another . . . it seems to me I do this out of curiosity, I have to be looking everywhere. It seems to me that it is to see evil. I don't know if you will understand me. . . . How do you expect me to receive Holy Communion tomorrow and Friday?"[127] Thérèse was certain sanctity did not mean self-torment. She wrote right away with all her energy trained on Marie's problem.

> You did well to write to me, and I understand *everything . . . everything, everything, everything!* . . . You haven't committed *the shadow of any evil;* I know what these kinds of temptations are so well that I can assure you of this without any fear . . . pay no attention whatsoever to them. . . . I hear you saying to me: 'Thérèse is saying this because she doesn't know . . . she doesn't know I really do it on purpose . . . it pleases me. . . . Yes . . . Thérèse does know; I tell you that she understands it *all . . .* she too has passed through the *martyrdom* of scruples. . . .[128]

During meditation, the one moment of the day when she might expect quiet, Thérèse sat in front of a nun who clicked her teeth. Thérèse perspired; she fought it, but she could not ignore it. "I had the great desire," she wrote, "to turn my head and stare at the culprit who was very certainly unaware of her 'click.' " She finally gave up trying to pray, and simply sat and listened to the "click."[129] Another time she entered her cell to find that its sole attractive item, a dainty water jug, was missing and replaced by a larger, less graceful one, *"all chipped."*[130] And then there was Sister St.-Pierre.

While she was a novice Thérèse volunteered to help the elderly nun to dinner each evening. At 10 minutes to 6:00 Sister St.-Pierre would shake her hourglass and Thérèse would rise. Her task was to

... carry her little bench in a certain way, above all I was not to hurry, and then the walk took place. It was a question of following the poor invalid by holding her cincture; ... if by mistake she took a false step, immediately it appeared to her that I was holding her incorrectly and that she was about to fall. "Ah! My God! You are going too fast; I'm going to break something." If I tried to go more slowly, "Well, come on! I don't feel your hand; you've let me go and I'm going to fall! Ah, I was right when I said you were too young to help me."[131]

Once she had settled her in the refectory Thérèse was free to leave Sister St.-Pierre, but she began to notice how painfully the crippled hands worked at the piece of bread. Irascible or not, abusive or not, Sister St.-Pierre was quite alone and struggling. Thérèse decided to begin staying another minute to cut the old nun's bread and to leave her with a smile.[132]

As the months passed and Mr. Martin became more and more withdrawn and helpless, any hope that he might return to Les Buissonnets was extinguished. Because of repairs on the speakroom, Thérèse and Céline talked over the plans to break up the household in the convent confessional box.[133] Thérèse wrote to Marie, "Life will pass very quickly. In heaven it will make no difference to us when we see that all the *relics* of Les Buissonnets have been carried off here and there!"[134] Brave words, but written at a distance from the "relics" themselves.

One late October day the wagons loaded with old pieces of furniture from the Martin home rolled into the Carmel courtyard. Thérèse was steeled to see the furniture, but not her old spaniel dog, Tom, who had followed the wagons down the hill. Céline described the scene: "Once inside the cloister, the faithful Tom raised his ears, then, looking in all directions as if to get his bearings, he sprang on his little mistress . . . leaping up at her face and making a thousand bounds in all directions. She was obliged to lift her large veil and hide Tom under it, for he could not control his joy. . . . She was forced to tear herself away from all this. . . .''[135] The lease on Les Buissonnets ended on Christmas Day.[136] The break was complete.

In the choir of the Carmel Louis Martin's clock now tolled the hours.[137] Also in the choir hung a picture of the face of the suffering Christ, one based on the old tradition that as He made His way up the hill of Calvary a woman named Veronica had wiped the sweat and blood from Jesus' face and found that face imprinted on her veil.[138] On the day she took her habit Thérèse of the Child Jesus had made a significant change in her name — she added the words, "of the Holy Face."[139] During the dark days of 1889 and 1890 in a convent steeped in abstract, elaborate prayers, mortification and the justice of a stern God, Thérèse turned to one strong, concrete, personal image: the human face of the suffering Christ. In the fall of 1889 as Sister Martha of Jesus watched, Thérèse stopped sweeping the public chapel long enough to mount the altar steps and knock on the Tabernacle door. "Are You there, Jesus?" she asked. "Answer me, I beg you."[140]

Pervading Thérèse's letters now is the wish to live "hidden," "unknown," "forgotten," by all but "Him."[141] Often she called herself "the grain of sand."[142] In the Old Testament Thérèse found a passage from the prophet Isaiah that fit her own unembroidered idea of the human Christ. In the summer of 1890 she copied out for Céline the Fourth Song of the Suffering Servant:

> Who would believe what we have heard? To whom has the arm of the Lord been revealed? The Christ will grow up like a sapling before the Lord and like a shoot that comes from a parched

soil. He is without beauty and without stately bearing; we have seen him; he had nothing that would attract our eyes and we despised him. He appeared to us as an object of scorn, the least of men, a man of sorrows, acquainted with suffering! . . . His face is as though hidden! . . . He seemed to be despicable, and we did not recognize him. . . . He truly took our infirmities upon himself, and he was burdened with our offenses. We looked upon him as a leper, as a man struck by God and humbled! . . . And yet he was pierced through for our iniquities, he was broken for our crimes. The chastisement which was to procure our peace fell upon him, and we were healed by his wounds.[143]

Thérèse's final vows were set for September 1890. She was 17.

THE ELEVATOR

The day she received the Carmelite habit Thérèse had dressed as a bride, but the Ceremony of Profession was the real wedding. To prepare to take her lifelong vows in September 1890, Thérèse once more withdrew for a retreat, this time for 10 days. Once more she felt "tired of earthly consolations."[1] "I don't understand the retreat I am making," she wrote to Pauline a week before the Profession. "I think of nothing, in a word, I am in a very dark subterranean passage!"[2] Two days later she wrote that "at the bottom of my soul I feel that there will be a day of DISTANCES, infinite DISTANCES that will make me forget forever the sorrows of the desert and the exile."[3] Yet Thérèse claimed still to be at peace. "My soul is always in the subterranean passage, but it is *very happy.*"[4]

The night before her profession,

> . . . a storm arose within my soul the like of which I'd never seen before. Not a single doubt concerning my vocation had ever entered my mind until then . . . my vocation appeared to me as a *dream*, a chimera. I found life in Carmel to be very beautiful, but . . . it wasn't for me. . . . I was misleading my Superiors . . . the darkness was so great that I could see and understood one thing only: I didn't have a vocation.[5]

Certain that her novice-mistress would stop the profession

if she knew, Thérèse nonetheless beckoned Sister Marie of the Angels out of the choir. Talking calmed her, and so did Sister Marie. Then Thérèse faced Mother Gonzague, who "simply laughed at me. . . . In the morning . . . I felt as though I were flooded with a river of peace."[6] The Carmel was less serene than Thérèse. According to Pauline, the nuns arose that morning to the sound of "thousands of swallows . . . chirping . . . on all our roofs. Never before had we seen such an army of these little emigrants."[7]

All outsiders are banned from the Ceremony of Profession. With the community as witnesses, Thérèse prostrated herself in front of Mother Gonzague on a flower-rimmed rug in the center of the chapter room.[8] She had written her promises on a little slip of paper — the *billet de profession* — which would be buried with her. She vowed to live as a Carmelite until her death. "May I never seek nor find anything but Yourself alone. May creatures be nothing for me and may I be nothing for them, but may You, Jesus, be *everything*! May the things of earth never be able to trouble my soul, and may nothing disturb my peace. Jesus, I ask You for nothing but peace, and also love, infinite love without any limits other than Yourself. . . . Give me martyrdom of heart or of body, or rather give me both."[9] At the urging of her sisters she also said a special prayer that day for her father: "My God, I beg You, may it be Your will that Papa be cured."[10] The next day Mother Gonzague wrote to the Carmel of Tours, "This angelic child is only seventeen and a half, and she has the judgment of one of thirty, the religious perfection of an old perfected novice, and possession of herself; she is a perfect religious. Yesterday not an eye remained dry. . . ."[11]

The final stage of the profession was the taking of the black veil in a public ceremony two weeks later. This time there was no river of peace but a flood of tears. Her father's humiliating illness constantly plagued Thérèse. Louis was now helpless. Six months earlier, a nun at the mental hospital had written Céline, "His limbs cannot support him. Monsieur Martin does not leave his bed. If you are living in an isolated spot, I would advise you to take him, for he is not difficult to handle. . . . Your good father does not even try to wash himself.''[12] The family did not bring Louis home. By September he had improved a little.

Thérèse longed to see her father on her big day, and she and Céline plotted across the grilles to bring Louis to Lisieux. On Tuesday morning, the day before the ceremony, Céline suggested that she bring Louis to only part of it to avoid tiring him. "At the end . . . I will go and get him, and I will bring him quietly up to the grille.''[13] There he would bless Thérèse. The little plot was crushed on Tuesday afternoon when Isidore Guérin appeared in the speakroom.[14]

On Wednesday Thérèse disrupted the Carmel. Louis would not be there, Father Pichon was in Canada, even the bishop had gotten sick. She cried like an orphan. Her tears annoyed the nuns, who imagined the public reaction to seeing the black veil of their order lowered onto the head of a weeping 17-year-old. "I can't understand your crying!'' snapped an irritated Pauline as the procession moved toward the chapel. "How can you hope to have our Father at your ceremony?'' Thérèse's tears ruffled the patience of even gentle Mother Geneviève, too sick to attend, who sent "a very severe reprimand.''[15]

A local pharmacist and friend of the Guérins, Monsieur Lahaye, witnessed Thérèse's taking of the black veil.

> During her profession ceremony, I was standing in the sanctuary and could see her behind the grille. The black veil she was going to receive was covered with a crown of roses and lying on the altar. The white veil she was still wearing had been raised, and I could see the fine symmetry of her features . . . her forehead was slightly convex, the nose short, the mouth

almost large, the chin quite large and rounded
. . . her cheekbones were a little prominent . . .
she seemed slender despite her heavy religious
habit.[16]

One other feature struck Monsieur Lahaye. Thérèse's
eyes, which normally had a "natural gentleness," he said,
on that day showed "a certain gravity."[17]

Hidden away in the Lisieux Carmel Thérèse found
emptiness, loss, pain, isolation and, she insisted, peace.
She said she was happy. The same paradox imbues the
writings of the Spanish Carmelite priest-poet who was a
contemporary of Teresa of Avila 300 years earlier. John of
the Cross's step-by-step path up the mountain to spiritual
union with God reads at times like a road map of Thérèse's young life.

A contemplative aims at an inner union with God but
cannot effect this union simply by willing it, said John,
even in the harsh life of the cloister. Nor was the union the
same as high feelings, or accomplished by bizarre
penances or extreme ascetic practices, as beginners in the
spiritual life often thought. Beginners are drawn to "relics
and medals, like children with coral."[18] Some decorate
places of prayer. This, too, failed. "The pleasure which
they set upon their painted adornments is stolen from the
living reality."[19]

Only God can transform a soul, said John. But the person must prepare, must cooperate by removing the "fat of
the soul." This means purging oneself of attachment to all
objects, all people, all emotions, and also by accepting the
purging that is sent, such as the illness or death of someone you love. The example is Job. But this total purging
does not effect union with God. Quite the opposite. The immediate effect of the purging of the senses is terror. Without its human comforts the soul is left in a void, "not only
in darkness, but in emptiness."[20] For John, if the self is at-

tached to anything at all — be it another person, a costly crucifix, a holy picture, a nostalgic memory, the arrangement of a room, or even a ritual way of passing a day — this attachment "is an anxiety that, like a bond, ties the spirit down to the earth and allows it no enlargement of heart."[21] The central obstacle to spiritual freedom is not things themselves but craving, anxiety, the feeling of attachment and fear of loss which grips the heart.

When finally cleansed, the self is naked. And how does it feel? "Arid," said John, "empty . . . like a barren and dry land." The soul is isolated, hidden in "a wild and vast solitude." But the dark night produces other effects as well — liberty of spirit, the death of anxiety, a growth in patience toward others, a greater capacity to absorb suffering, and, for some, an inability to explain to a spiritual director what is going on within them. Finally, there is a certain peace. "In a dark night . . . / Forth unobserved I went, / My house being now at rest."[22]

But the night of sense is only the first stage of purgation. More terrible is the night of the spirit. When the "deep caverns of sense" are empty of natural affection but not yet filled with God, the soul believes "that God has abandoned it, of which it has no doubt; that He has cast it away into darkness as an abominable thing."[23] Only a very few pass through the agony of the night of the spirit. It is like suffocation. Beyond it, and only beyond it, lies contemplative union with God which John describes in his poetry as a "living flame of love." The soul is "wounded . . . burned" with a love so powerful, so far beyond any human attachment, that it longs for an end to life on earth. "I die," he said, "because I do not die." These souls, said John, tend to die young.

While talk of the writings of Teresa Avila saturated the Carmel's air, John of the Cross was seldom read; in fact he was hardly known then in France. Once Thérèse discovered him — at the age of 17 — for the next one or two years she read little else.

John did not teach a God offended by a teenager dozing off during early morning Mass. He did not teach a God who expected guilt over trivial faults or exacted harsh bodily mortifications. The severe and just Lord of ascetics who were bent on humiliation and punishing their flesh was not John's God. He wrote not of abasing the self but of emptying the self of all attachments that cause anxiety, that weigh down the spirit. The summer before her profession, Thérèse copied for Céline a fragment of one of John's poems:

> I abandoned and forgot myself
> Laying my face on my Beloved;
> All things ceased; I went out from myself,
> Leaving my cares
> Forgotten among the lilies.[24]

John of the Cross was called a mystic. The word was not used in the sense of an uplifting thrill from the sun sinking in the mountains, of a fleeting emotional moment, or even a feeling that God is near. The word's meaning was precise. Mystical union for John was the result of God's choosing a spiritual fusion with a particular human soul. It was rare. Most significantly, this mystical union cost the chosen soul. It cost dearly. No one could share union with God, no one could experience this spiritual transformation, unless he or she first passed through the dark night of the soul.

The heroic tradition of sanctity seemed to have little in common with Thérèse's daily existence. The lives of the saints read aloud in the refectory were written in abstract and pious language to accent extraordinary feats, not to reveal the human touches of a real life. By comparison, Thérèse's existence was not very grand at all. She faced a paradox. She wanted to be a saint so she could share life with God, but was struggling just to avoid suffocation under the irritations and pain of each ordinary day — the chipped jug left in her cell, Sister St. Vincent de Paul's bit-ing tongue, the letter that said that her father could no longer wash himself. She had entered Carmel with the high ideal of sacrificing her own life for other souls, yet she could not finish her assigned sewing and at times could not even keep awake during the Mass. What must God think of her? As she had done when she was a student at the Benedictine Abbey and spent her free time thinking in the alcove behind her bed, Thérèse reflected.

She tested her thoughts on a Jesuit priest who preached a retreat at the Carmel about the time of her profession. According to Pauline, Thérèse told Father Blino that she wanted to be a saint, "to love God as much as St. Teresa (of Avila)." "Pride," the priest charged, "presumption." He advised the young nun to "confine yourself to correcting your faults, to offending God no longer, to making a little progress in virtue each day, and temper your rash desires." Thérèse did not consider her desires to be a saint, even a great saint, rash. "See, Father," she said, "how vast the field is, and it seems to me I have the right to run in it." She failed to persuade Father Blino.[25]

Thérèse was troubled the day she visited Mother Geneviève, in her eighties now and confined to bed. Finding the limit of two visitors already in the room, Thérèse smiled and turned to leave. Mother Geneviève stopped her and told her that she should "serve God with peace and joy." She quoted St. Paul — "Our God is a God of peace."[26] The words shot to the heart of Thérèse's conflict. She hurried back the following Sunday to find out if Mother Geneviève had received a revelation about her from God. Revelation? No, said the simple nun, not at all. She had had no revelation. Thérèse saw a lesson here. Mother Geneviève was honest, direct, devoid of affectation. Thérèse wanted to imitate this style of sanctity "because in it one meets with no deceptions."[27]

The year after her profession Thérèse finally met a priest who understood her. Father Alexis Prou, a 47-year-old Franciscan, came to the Carmel to preach a retreat in the fall of 1891. "At the time I was having great interior trials of all kinds," she wrote, "even to the point of asking myself whether heaven really existed. I felt disposed to say nothing . . . since I didn't know how to express them."[28] When she began her confession to Father Alexis, all the torment poured out. Quite simply, Thérèse wanted to cast off all the fears, all the anxiety about offending God, and approach Him with "confidence and love." Father Alexis dismissed the teaching that filled the air that her faults offended God. God was pleased with her, he said. The faults of a human being could not hurt God. This was news to Thérèse, and precisely what she needed. "Never had I heard that our faults *could not cause God any pain*. . . . My nature was such that fear made me recoil." "He launched me full sail upon the waves of *confidence and love*."[29] Finally she had found a priest who understood her. She asked permission to speak again with Father Alexis, who was available for conferences during the retreat. Mother Gonzague refused.[30]

Death in the cloister was a public event to be shared with those who had shared one's life. When the bell summoned the sisters to the infirmary on Saturday, December 5, 1891, Thérèse was placed at the foot of Mother Geneviève's bed.[31] Clustered in the little room at the corner of the cloister, the sisters prayed and watched for two hours as their foundress lay dying. Thérèse was 18. Fourteen years had passed since her first and only sight of death, and watching this death unlocked the memory of the first. Mother Geneviève's coffin reminded her of her mother's. "It was similar in size. I imagined myself back once again in the days of my childhood and all those memories flooded into my mind . . . the coffin appeared *smaller*. I had no need *to raise* my head to see."[32]

Only a few weeks later, death became a common sight when the influenza epidemic that had spread death across

France finally invaded the cloister. It struck in January. One nun died on Thérèse's 19th birthday, two others shortly afterward,[33] and Thérèse found she could face a lifeless body without any fear, even alone in the dark. "Death reigned supreme. The ones who were most ill were taken care of by those who could scarcely drag themselves around. As soon as a Sister breathed her last, we were obliged to leave her alone. One morning upon arising I had a presentiment that Sister Magdalene was dead; the dormitory was in darkness, and no one was coming out of the cells. I decided to enter Sister Magdalene's cell, since the door was wide open. I saw her fully dressed and lying across her bed." On her own Thérèse brought the customary wreath of roses and candle back to the dead nun's cell.[34]

More painful for Thérèse was the relentless living death of her father. Louis was meek, wept easily, and withdrew more and more, often covering his head with his handkerchief.[35] Finally, in May of 1892, he came home to Lisieux to die. Three years had passed since the day he stood in the Carmel speakroom and showed Pauline a couple of little fish. Two days after he got home a very weak and childlike Louis was wheeled into the Carmel parlor. He could not speak, but as he was being wheeled out Louis managed two simple words, "in heaven."[36] Thérèse never saw him again.

The tone of life in the Carmel at Lisieux at that point is described by Sister Mary Magdalene, who joined the Lisieux Carmelites two months after Louis's last visit. She ". . . found the community in a very disappointing state. I used to think all Carmelite nuns were saints, but I gradually became aware that at the time there were a lot of very imperfect nuns. They were noticeably lacking in silence, regularity, and especially mutual charity, and there were some lamentable divisions among them."[37]

Though Thérèse took no part in the rivalry, the hostility of some of the opponents of the Martin faction extended to her. According to Sister Mary Magdalene, "about half of them said she was a good little nun, a gentle person, but that she had never had to suffer and that her life had been rather insignificant. The other half were affected by the party animosity . . . so their view was more unfavorable. These said she had been spoiled by her sisters."[38] What this animosity meant in daily living is clear from an incident described by Sister Mary Magdalene. "There was one sister in the kitchen who did not like . . . (Thérèse) and spoke of her with contempt. . . . Once, when she saw Sister Thérèse coming, she said: 'Look at the walk of her! She's not in any hurry. When is she going to start working? She's good for nothing.' Sister Thérèse heard her, but when she came in she gave this sister a big smile."[39]

In 1893 Pauline Martin became prioress of the Carmel.[40] The new, young prioress — Pauline was only 31, Mother Gonzague nearly 60 — faced an impossible first task, soothing her predecessor's aroused jealousy. Pauline appointed Mother Gonzague to the prestigious post of mistress of novices, but did not want her actually training the young nuns. One nun in the convent had remained apart from the political rivalry — Thérèse. Since only two members of one family could be given full voting powers, Thérèse didn't even have a vote.[41] With the understanding that she should mollify the former prioress and dilute her influence on the young nuns, Pauline appointed Thérèse assistant to the mistress of novices.[42]

The 19-year-old Thérèse taught and directed two novices. Sister Mary Magdalene, was one of 11 children and as a very young child had been sent away from her crowded home to work, and was attacked. Though intelligent when she joined the community at age 22, Sister Mary Magdalene was still wounded by her early years. So withdrawn and sullen was she that the community nearly sent her away.[43] The other novice, Sister Martha of Jesus, was eight years older than Thérèse and had joined the community three months earlier, yet she remained a novice. She was insecure, jealous, with a harsh temper, and it was she who had served leftovers to Thérèse. Their descriptions of Thérèse in her new office also suggest how hard they made her job. Sister Martha of Jesus:

> I was sometimes a bit jealous, and would get angry when she called attention to my shortcomings. . . . I used to go away and refuse to speak to her. . . .
> One day I was upset and said some very hurtful things to her. She just went on talking calmly and gently, asking me to help her with some work she had to do. I gave in, still muttering to myself at the inconvenience she was causing me. Then I thought I would see how far her patience could be stretched, so . . . I decided not to answer when she spoke to me. But I failed to upset her. . . . Sister Thérèse did not scold me, nor did she say a word to hurt me. . . .[44]

Sister Mary Magdelene:

> I never felt any natural affection for her. I even avoided her. . . . Still she did not desert me. . . . Whenever I was depressed she went out of her way to distract me and cheer me up. . . . When it was my turn to wash up, she often arranged things so that she could work beside me and chat to me. She showed trust in me. . . .[45]

They both came to admire her, and Sister Martha of Jesus later testified: "Everything about her commanded respect."[46] More surprising was the growing esteem of Mother Gonzague. In a letter to another convent, written the year she became novice mistress, Mother Gonzague described Thérèse:

88

Tall and strong, with the air of a child, with a tone of voice and an expression that hide in her the wisdom, perfection and perspicacity of a fifty-year-old . . . a little "untouchable saint," to whom you would give the Good God without confession, but whose cap is full of mischief to play on whomever she wants. A mystic, a comic, she is everything. She can make you weep with devotion and just as easily faint with laughing during recreation.[47]

In June of 1894, the year after Thérèse had assumed her new duties, she suffered from a chronic sore throat, chest pain and a hoarse voice. The family was sufficiently concerned that Francis La Néele, Jeanne Guérin's husband and a medical doctor, examined Thérèse briefly. Though her sore throat, cough and hoarseness persisted into the fall — as did the Guérin's concern[48] — Thérèse's attention focused not on her throat, but on the major event of the summer. In July, after what she termed "a death of five years," Louis Martin died. In September Céline joined her sisters at the Carmel.

Céline was a painter, a photographer, a dreamer — impulsive, emotional, bright, impatient, and six and a half years behind Thérèse in starting her religious life. She burst into the Carmel with her "irresistable drive" and set out to be a perfect nun. Her immediate superior, the assistant novice mistress, told her that she had not come to Carmel "to turn out a mountain of work." Work like the Israelites building the walls of Jerusalem, cautioned Thérèse, with a sword in one hand to hold off whatever attacked her inner peace.[49] And she shouldn't go to extremes with bodily penances. That was self-punishment, not love. She should confine herself to what was permitted by the Rule. When Céline was exhausted by her efforts and depressed, Thérèse told her that what she needed was not heroics but humility.[50]

Céline's breathless pursuit of perfection and her "mortifications" were rooted in the heroic tradition of sanctity. Thérèse had been slowly carving out another way, rooted not in grand deeds, asceticism and the image of a God who exacts perfection, but in avoiding all self-seeking, in unseen acts of personal kindness within the grasp of an ordinary soul, and a God whom she could trust to love her despite her flaws. She sought a "means of going to heaven by a little way, a way that . . . (was) very straight, very short, and totally new." As she explained her thought, "We are living now in an age of inventions, and we no longer have to take the trouble of climbing stairs, for in the homes of the rich, an elevator has replaced these very successfully. I wanted to find an elevator which would raise me to Jesus, for I am too small to climb the rough stairway of perfection."[51]

Céline arrived in the Carmel toting an elaborate new camera and a manuscript of much of the Old Testament which she had copied by hand from her uncle's Bibles. The camera she kept to photograph the sisters of the hidden community. The Old Testament she gave to Thérèse.

Except for the extracts used in prayer and readings in the Carmel, Thérèse had no access to the Old Testament.[52] In Céline's manuscript Thérèse found what she was looking for — a scriptural basis for her own "little way."

> I searched, then, in the Scriptures for some sign of this elevator, the object of my desires, and I read these words coming from the mouth of Eternal Wisdom: *"Whoever is a LITTLE ONE, let him come to me."* And so I succeeded. I felt I had found what I was looking for. But wanting to know, O my God, what you would do to *the very little one* who answered Your call, I continued my search and this is what I discovered: *"As one whom a mother caresses, so will I comfort you; you shall*

Above: Zélie and Louis Joseph Martin, Thérèse's parents

Left: Celine, left, was 12 when this photo was taken; Thérèse was 8

Facing page: The Martin sisters posed with their prioress. Seated from left: Mother Marie de Gonzague, Marie and Thérèse. Standing: Celine and Pauline

Thérèse was 22 when she portrayed Joan of Arc in a drama staged in the convent on Mother Agnes' feast day.

In the July 1895 photo at left, Thérèse (left) is shown doing her laundry in the primitive style of the late 1800s

Raking hay was a project involving all the Carmelites. Thérèse is
at left rear

Photos at right show the convent's refectory, Thérèse's seat in the
chapel and her cell. The cell had no heat and the bed was the type
found in peasant cottages: wood planks laid across a trestle and
covered with a canvas bag of straw

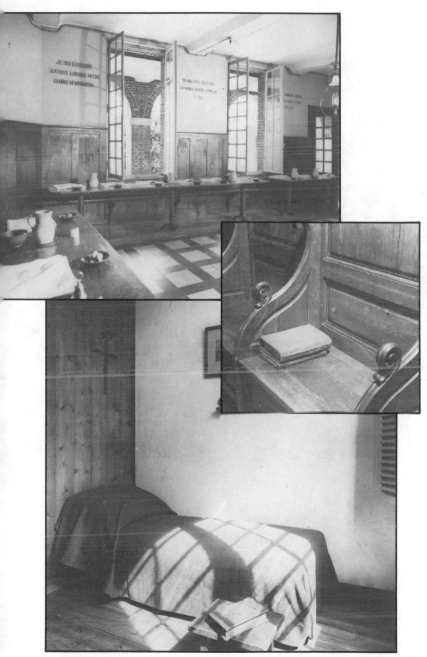

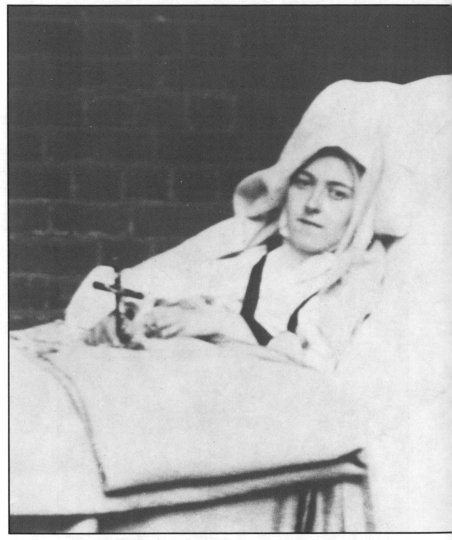

Even on her death bed, Thérèse's face did not reveal the extent to which tuberculosis ravaged her body

be carried at the breasts, and upon the knees they shall caress you.[53]

Thérèse now read and reread the books Céline had copied. She compared the translation with the extracts she knew from the Divine Office and the readings in the choir and the refectory. Raised in a tradition hesitant about personal interpretation of the Bible, Thérèse nonetheless interpreted passages of the Old Testament for Céline:

> Is this such a fast as I have chosen: for a man to afflict his soul for a day? . . . that he put on sackcloth and ashes? Wilt thou call this a fast and a day acceptable to the Lord? Is not this rather the fast that I have chosen? Loose the bands of wickedness, undo the bundles that oppress, let them that are broken go free and break asunder every burden. Deal thy bread to the hungry and bring the needy and the harborless into thy house; when thou shalt see one naked, clothe him, and despise not thine own flesh. . . .[54]

Isaiah's words were generally taken literally, but the obligation became frequently an abstract act — a donation of money for the needy. Thérèse saw the poor, the hungry, the naked right there in the Carmel. They were Sister St. Pierre, Sister Mary Magdalene, Sister Martha of Jesus, Mother Gonzague — maimed and twisted people whose hunger and poverty and sickness was in their souls. The obligation to care for them was as strong as to feed a starving child. "We are surrounded, . . ." she told Céline, "by . . . souls in need, by weak souls and souls that are sick and oppressed . . . share your substance with the poor . . . open up your house and part with your possessions. In other words, make a complete sacrifice of your rest and tranquility."[55] If the effort remains discreet, hidden, "the prophet promises that *you will recover your health of mind.*"[56]

Céline, who had had to praise the 14-year-old Thérèse like a child when she made a bed at home, now observed her sister "open her house and part with her possessions." Thérèse had become the poet of the convent, and all the nuns wanted a poem for their feast days. "Her 'silences' and her Sundays were spent, more often than not," says Céline, "writing poems at the request of other sisters. She never refused anybody."[57] Thérèse did not take the time to make copies of the poems for herself. She volunteered for jobs with the nuns who were depressed or hard to get along with, such as Sister Mary Magdalene, and often spent her recreation with Sister Teresa of St. Augustine, whose personality she found grating. Thérèse concealed her revulsion so successfully that Céline thought Sister Teresa of Augustine was a close friend of her sister's.[58] Thérèse, it seems, did not even safeguard her annual retreat. She took it with Sister Martha of Jesus and agreed to Sister Martha's method of keeping a total of her daily charitable acts and sacrifices.[59]

One night around Christmas 1894, not long after Céline had entered the Carmel, the Martin sisters were all warming themselves by the fireplace in the recreation room. Thérèse was entertaining her sisters with old family stories. Marie said, "What a pity we haven't got all that in writing."

"I couldn't ask for anything better," Pauline said, and Thérèse laughed.

"I order you," said Pauline, "to write down all your childhood memories."[60] Pauline allotted no time for the task. Throughout the year 1895 in her free time during Silences and on Sundays, Thérèse sat in her cell, the portable writing table on her lap, and roamed the paths of her memory. She wrote her most intimate memories, just for Pauline.

As she jotted down these memories, Thérèse did not write in the unnatural handwriting taught to her at home

100

and at the Benedictine abbey. She wrote, as she thought, in an unaffected, unslanted style.[61]

Thérèse laid down no abstract formula for a virtuous life but retraced her steps toward her little way in a vivid, concrete mosaic of the people, the landscape, the events, the thoughts, the reading that had shaped her. When Thérèse was small, Pauline had often spoken to her in the language of flowers. Now Thérèse framed the story of her soul, as she called it, with this language she shared with Pauline. "He willed to create great souls comparable to lilies and roses, but He has created smaller ones and these must be content to be daisies or violets."[62] Hers was the story not of one of the grand and elegant lilies of creation but of a little flower, with emphasis on the world *little*.

Thérèse quoted letters from her mother about the "little imp," memories of Sunday walks in Alençon through "fields enameled with *cornflowers*."[63] She recalled the spot in her mother's bedroom where she had stood by Céline's side to watch Zélie die, and Jeanne and Marie Guérin waiting at the door after the train trip to Lisieux. She remembered Isidore Guérin singing "Blue Beard" with her perched on his knees and Louis rocking her by the fire. Throughout the story Thérèse wrote of nature — flowers, the sea at Trouville, the mountains in Switzerland; nature pervaded even her dreams. "I dream usually about such things as woods, flowers, streams and the sea; I see beautiful children almost all the time; I catch butterflies and birds the like of which I've never seen before."[64] The story reveals a clear, observant mind that judged from experience and recalled sense impressions in detail. Writing for Pauline, Thérèse concealed nothing — the gargoyles are there as well as the flowers. But the tone of her story is tender, not bitter, and it builds to a childlike trust in God.

In the old sermons and meditations bound together in *The Treasure of the Carmel* was contained the idea of offering oneself as a victim to God's justice to atone for the sins of humanity.[65] The story of one such victim was read aloud in the refectory in 1894. Sister Marie of the Cross, one of the Lisieux Carmelites who had suffered for 33 years before dying in 1882, reportedly offered herself to God's justice. So, it was said, had Mother Geneviève.[66]

As she knelt behind the grille for Mass on Sunday the 9th of June, Thérèse was thinking about these people who called down on themselves punishments for sinners in order to satisfy the justice of God. The idea held no appeal for her. Thérèse was struck not with God's exacting justice, but with His love, given freely even though in the scramble for happiness people rejected it, indeed, ignored it. "Oh my God!" she prayed. "Is Your disdained love going to remain closed up within Your Heart? It seems to me that if You were to find souls offering themselves as victims of holocaust to Your love, You would consume them rapidly; it seems to me too, that You would be happy not to hold back the waves of infinite tenderness within You...."[67]

Motioning to Céline, Thérèse left the choir and followed Pauline to the turnstyle. Would it be all right, Thérèse asked her prioress, if she offered herself to God's love? Embarrassed, she explained a little of her thinking. With the air of the Carmel saturated with gothic prayers, Pauline failed to single this one out. Yes, she said offhandedly, that would be all right. "Mother Agnes was busy," Céline explains, "and did not seem to understand too well what was going on."[68]

Thérèse drew up a formal offering and gave it to Pauline to be checked by a theologian. Two days after the conversation at the turnstyle, Thérèse and Céline knelt alone in a room adjoining Thérèse's cell[69] and Céline listened to her sister recite the "Offering of Myself as a Holocaust Victim to the Merciful Love of God." The Offering was intensely personal and precise. It reads in part:

102

O My God! . . . I desire to *Love* You and make You *Loved* . . . I desire, in a word, to be a saint, but I feel my helplessness and I beg You, O my God! to be Yourself my *Sanctity*!

Since You loved me so much as to give me Your only Son as my Savior and my Spouse, the infinite treasures of His merits are mine. I offer them to You with gladness. . . .

I am certain . . . that You will grant my desires. I know, O my God! that *the more You want to give, the more You make us desire.* I feel in my heart immense desires and it is with confidence I ask You to come and take possession of my soul. Ah! I cannot receive Holy Communion as often as I desire, but, Lord are You not *all-powerful*? Remain in me as in a tabernacle and never separate Yourself from Your little victim. . . .

I thank You, O my God! for all the graces You have granted me, especially the grace of making me pass through the crucible of suffering. . . .

After earth's Exile, I hope to go and enjoy You in the Fatherland, but I do not want to lay up merits for heaven. I want to work for Your *Love alone* with the one purpose of pleasing You. . . .

In the evening of this life, I shall appear before You with empty hands, for I do not ask You, Lord, to count my works. All our justice is stained in Your eyes. . . .

In order to live in one single act of perfect Love, I OFFER MYSELF AS A VICTIM OF HOLOCAUST TO YOUR MERCIFUL LOVE, asking You to consume me incessantly, allowing the waves of *infinite tenderness* shut up within You to overflow into my soul, and that thus I may become a *martyr* of Your *Love*, O my God!

May this martyrdom, after having prepared me to appear before You, finally cause me to die. . . .

I want . . . at each beat of my heart to renew this offering to You an infinite number of times, until the shadows having disappeared, I may be able to tell You of my *Love* in and Eternal *Face to Face!*[70]

"I let her do it," Pauline said later, "but attached no great importance to it."[71]

One day while Marie was out in the quadrangle raking grass, Thérèse asked her if she wanted to offer herself as a victim of God's love. "Indeed not," said the practical Marie, "for if I offered myself as a victim, God would take me at my word, and I have a great dread of suffering. Besides, far from inspiring me, the word *victim* has always repelled me."[72] Thérèse told Marie that this was not an offering to appease a just God, not a request for suffering, but an act of love to a personal God who was ignored. "She won me over," Marie said later. Marie made the offering, and so did another novice under Thérèse's direction, Sister Marie of the Trinity.[73]

As she passed the prioress's stall for evening prayer one night in January 1896, Thérèse slipped the copybook of her memories to Pauline, who simply nodded. Preoccupied with the coming elections — she was pitted against Mother Gonzague — Pauline put Thérèse's manuscript aside for another two months.[74] The distraction was understandable. Hoping to unseat Pauline, Mother Gonzague, the mistress of novices, tried to block Céline's Profession

104

until after the March elections. Her scheme failed, but her effort to manipulate the timing of sacred vows angered even Thérèse.[75]

The petty crusade, fought against the backdrop of the prayer and severe fast of Lent, ended two and one half weeks before Easter — with a double ceremony. According to the account in *le Normand*, the Martin family was center stage:

> Two rare and very touching ceremonies took place today in the pious and attractive chapel of the Carmel. Two amiable young women, united again in the closeness of their blood ties, two cousins, made a new commitment with God to consecrate themselves entirely to Him, to belong to Him without reservation. And there, near them, a father, a mother, uncle and aunt at the same time, of the sisters, made with most admirable abnegation the painful sacrifice that heaven demanded of them. For them the separation is cruel, the rending is profound; but their soul, elevated above aspirations and affections which are purely earthly, submits itself generously to the divine will. . . .

> This morning at 8:30, Mademoiselle Céline Martin, surrounded by three of her sisters who had preceeded her in monastic life, pronounced her final vows and took the veil of the professed. . . .

> This afternoon, at 3:00 o'clock, Mademoiselle Marie Guérin completed the first part of her novitiate and was clothed in the habit of the Carmel.[76]

The author of the article was Isidore Guérin.

The following Saturday the badly split community took seven ballots to choose their prioress.[77] When the election was over, Thérèse entered the choir and saw Mother Gonzague in the prioress's seat.[78]

THE DARK NIGHT

Lent culminated in the rituals of Holy Week. On Holy Thursday it was the custom to remove the Eucharist from the altar tabernacle and place it in a separate receptacle called, symbolically, the Tomb. Thérèse prayed at the Tomb until midnight and then went to her cell. "I had scarcely laid my head upon the pillow when I felt something like a bubbling stream mounting to my lips. I didn't know what it was, but I thought that perhaps I was going to die. . . . However, as . . . (the) lamp was extinguished, I told myself I would have to wait until the morning to be certain, for it seemed to me that it was blood I had coughed up. The morning was not long in coming; upon awakening I thought immediately of . . . (what) I had to learn, so I went over to the window. I was able to see that I was not mistaken."[1] She found her handkerchief soaked with blood and reported the incident dutifully to the new prioress, Mother Gonzague. Insisting that she was in no pain, Thérèse requested that she be given "nothing special."[2]

It was Good Friday, the day of the "black fast," when the nuns ate nothing but bread and water. Good Friday was also housecleaning day, and it struck Marie that Thérèse looked tired and pale. "I asked her what was the matter, as she appeared to be ill, and I offered to help her. But she just thanked me, and said nothing about the mishap."[3] One of Thérèse's novices, Sister Marie of the Trinity, also noticed Thérèse on Good Friday. "She fasted on bread and water like the rest of us. Besides, she continued to take part in the housecleaning. When I saw her washing a tiled floor, looking all pale and worn out, I . . . offered to do her work for her, but she would not hear of it. That evening she took the discipline[4] with us for the space of three *misereres.*"[5] Alone in her cell Friday night, Thérèse again coughed up blood.

Far from feeling frightened, Thérèse welcomed the hemorrhage as *"a sweet and distant murmur which announced the Bridegroom's arrival."*[6] In fact she felt excited. "Never did Carmel's austerities appear so delightful to me; the hope of going to heaven soon transported me with joy."[7] Thérèse's joy was rooted in her belief that life was truly an exile that was now approaching an end. She was headed for her Homeland. An afterlife was not just a possibility, it was a certainty. "At this time I was enjoying such a living faith, such a clear *faith,* that the thought of heaven made up all my happiness."[8] Serious doubt was so foreign to Thérèse that she thought those who denied heaven's existence denied their own "inner convictions."[9]

During Easter week she learned otherwise. Within days of her excited reaction to the thought of a young death Thérèse was

> invaded by the thickest darkness . . . the thought of heaven, up until then so sweet to me, . . . (became) no longer anything but the cause of struggle and torment. . . . One would have to travel through this dark tunnel to understand its darkness. I will try to explain it by a comparison.
>
> I imagine I was born in a country which is covered in a thick fog. I never had the experience . . . of nature flooded . . . by the sun . . . from childhood I have heard people speak of these marvels and I know the country in which I am living is not really my true fatherland. . . .

This is not simply a story invented by someone living in the sad country where I am, but it is a reality, for the King of the Fatherland . . . came and lived for thirty-three years in the land of darkness . . . the certainty of going away one day from the sad and dark country has been given me from the day of my childhood. I did not believe this only because I heard it. . . . But I felt in the bottom of my heart real longings. . . .

. . . Suddenly the fog which surrounds me becomes more dense, it penetrates my soul and envelops it in such a way that it is impossible to discover within it the sweet image of my Fatherland; everything has disappeared! When I want to rest my heart fatigued by the darkness . . . by the memory of the luminous country . . . my torment redoubles; it seems to me that the darkness . . . says mockingly to me: "You are dreaming about the light . . . you are dreaming about the *eternal* possession of the Creator . . . you believe that one day you will walk out of this fog which surrounds you! Advance, advance; rejoice in death which will give you not what you hope for but a night still more profound, the night of nothingness."[10]

In 19th-century Europe the spitting of blood usually stirred terror. It was a classic symptom of tuberculosis. While Thérèse was in the Carmel tuberculosis struck about 150,000 French people each year. In the north of France, where she lived, the death rate ran about 500 per 100,000 inhabitants. The disease most often struck those between 21 and 35 years of age.[11] Though some victims experienced long stretches of remission, there was as yet no effective cure. The treatment that did exist depended on accurate diagnosis.

A common belief among doctors in the 19th century

was that pulmonary phthisis — the wasting away of the lungs — was often distinct from tuberculosis. Chronic lung inflammation, it was thought, caused the increase of mucus. In 1882 that theory was proven false. A German scientist named Robert Koch proved by experiments that a bacillus caused TB. The disease was not inherited but contagious, and all forms were related, whether in the lungs, brain or intestines. The destruction of lung tissue, chronic inflammation, the wasting away called consumption, were all due to the same cause — the TB bacillus.[12]

In the case of pulmonary tuberculosis, small tubercles lodged in the lung tissue, clustered, and softened into a yellow mass often described as cheese-like. As tubercles spread, lung tissue became inflamed and was destroyed while the patient experienced weight loss, fever, night sweating, chronic cough and, in later phases, spitting of blood. Death from TB is painful. As lung tissue erodes, the victim goes through something akin to suffocation.

In Thérèse's day TB was often difficult to diagnose in its early stages. The patient might appear healthy and the newly discovered X-ray was not yet in general use as a diagnostic tool.[13] Doctors relied heavily on the physical examination. In the early part of the century a French scientist named Laënnec had made the physical examination far more precise be developing the stethoscope. Laënnec wrote exact instructions for identifying breast sounds associated with tubercles, including rales and the echoing sound caused by cavities formed by the lesions.[14] He stressed the importance of tapping the chest and listening with the stethoscope to diagnose tuberculosis.

In a century and a place where the TB bacillus caused up to one third of middle-aged deaths,[15] it would scarcely seem possible to avoid considering TB in cases of chronic cough and spitting of blood. But some of the older generation of doctors, even in France, still clung to the discarded myth that what they called consumption, or the chronic lung inflammation of pulmonary phthisis, was not necessarily TB.[16] Rest and nutritious diet were generally accepted as important in treatment of TB, and Laënnec had also advocated fresh air. The wealthy sought the milder climates of southern France and Italy or moved into a sanitorium for a rest and fresh-air "cure."

The Guérins certainly could afford a sanitorium. By this time they had inherited a small fortune; Isidore had retired from the pharmacy, and they owned two elegant homes. According to one young visitor to La Musse, their summer chateau, "even the keys were gilded."[17] Thérèse's persistent sore throat and hoarseness had troubled her aunt and uncle since 1894, but they were separated from her by brick walls.

After Lent 1896, Dr. Francis La Néele, the Guérins' son-in-law, was permitted to examine Thérèse. The nun was on one side of the oratory grille, the doctor on the other, and she leaned her head through the opening. Francis La Néele apparently heard no distinctive sounds suggesting lesions or cavities — though Thérèse was, in fact, suffering from tuberculosis. That he failed to detect abnormal sounds is not surprising, for he listened through her thick wool habit. Dr. La Néele concluded that the blood she coughed up sprang from a ruptured blood vessel in her throat. He prescribed coating the throat with creosote, breathing in vapor and rubdowns with camphorated oil.[18] Had Thérèse been living the upper middle class French life of the Guérins, she would doubtlessly have been bundled off to the country or to the mountains. That those around her did not advocate or apparently consider such a move was not due to lack of concern but to the weight of the Carmelite vows. Thérèse had chosen to remain enclosed in the Carmel for life and to live as the poor.

In practical matters the sole authority over Thérèse was Mother Gonzague, and she did not choose to have Dr. La Néele act as Thérèse's physician. The prioress placed great faith in Dr. Alexandre de Cornière, the 55-year-old

111

physician to the Carmel who had practiced medicine for nearly 30 years. Dr. de Cornière had studied for a time at La Charité[19], the Paris hospital where in the early part of the century Laënnec had taught the importance of a proper examination. He was permitted to see Thérèse in the Carmel speakroom three months after she first coughed up blood. Though she had a persistent dry cough, the doctor was apparently not permitted to listen to breast sounds. In a letter to her aunt Thérèse described Dr. De Cornière's examination:

> You ask me, dear Aunt, to give you some news about my health just as I would to a "mother," and this I will do. But if I were to tell you I was doing marvelously well, you wouldn't believe me. So I will leave the word up to the celebrated Dr. de Cornière, to whom I had the *distinguished honor* of being presented yesterday in the speakroom. This illustrious personage, after have *honored* me with a look, declared *I was very well!*[20]

Since Dr. de Cornière did not hesitate to pronounce her fit on the basis of appearance, Thérèse continued rising at 5:00 a.m., eating a meatless diet, praying the Divine Office during the hours when she ran a fever, bending over the laundry pool to beat the wash with a wooden paddle, and breathing the linen room's steamy air.[21]

In September Marie asked a favor of Thérèse — that she jot down in a short note what Marie called the "little doctrine." A few days later she received three sheets of Thérèse's cramped writing.[22] What Marie read was a letter written for her but addressed, in part, to Jesus. An excerpt:

> Ah! my Jesus, pardon me if I am unreasonable in wishing to express my desires and longings which reach even unto infinity. Pardon

me and heal my soul by giving her what she longs for so much!

To be your *Spouse*, to be a *Carmelite*, and by my union with You to be the Mother of souls, should not this suffice me? And yet it is not so. No doubt, these three privileges sum up my true *vocation*: *Carmelite, Spouse, Mother*, and yet I feel within me other *vocations*. I feel the *vocation* of the WARRIOR, THE PRIEST, THE APOSTLE, THE DOCTOR, THE MARTYR. . . .

I feel in me the *vocation* of the PRIEST. . . . But alas! while desiring to be a *Priest*, I admire and envy the humility of St. Francis of Assisi and I feel the *vocation* of imitating him in refusing the sublime dignity of the *Priesthood*.

Oh Jesus, my Love, my Life, how can I combine these contrasts? How can I realize the desires of my poor *little soul*? . . .

Martyrdom was the dream of my youth, and this dream has grown with me within Carmel's cloisters. But here again, I feel that my dream is a folly, for I cannot confine myself to desiring *one kind* of martyrdom. To satisfy me I need *all* . . . I would be scourged and crucified. I would die flayed like St. Bartholomew. I would be plunged into boiling oil like St. John. . . .

O my Jesus! what is Your answer to all my follies? . . .

During my meditation, my desires caused me a veritable martyrdom, and I opened the Epistles of St. Paul to find some kind of answer. Chapters 12 and 13 of the First Epistle to the Corinthians fell under my eyes . . . *all* cannot be apostles, prophets, doctors. . . . The answer was clear, but it did not fulfill my desires and gave me no peace. . . . I continued my reading, and this sentence consoled me: *"Yet strive after THE BETTER GIFTS, and I point out to you a yet more excellent way."* And the Apostle explains how all *the most PERFECT gifts* are nothing without *LOVE.* That *Charity* is the EXCELLENT WAY that leads most surely to God. I finally had rest . . . *Charity* gave me the key to my *vocation.* . . . I understood that LOVE COMPRISED ALL VOCATIONS, THAT LOVE WAS EVERYTHING, THAT IT EMBRACED ALL TIMES AND PLACES . . . IN A WORD, THAT IT WAS ETERNAL!

. . . I cried out . . . my *vocation,* at last I have found it . . . MY VOCATION IS LOVE!

Yes, I have found my place in the Church, and it is You, O my God, who have given me this place; in the heart of the Church, My Mother, I shall be *Love.* . . .

I am only a child, powerless and weak, and yet it is my weakness that gives me the boldness of offering myself as *VICTIM of Your love, O Jesus!* In times past, victims, pure and spotless, were the only ones accepted by the Strong and Powerful God. To satisfy Divine *Justice,* perfect victims were necessary, but the *law of Love* has succeeded to the law of fear, and *Love* has chosen me as a holocaust, me, a weak and imperfect creature. Is not this choice worthy of *Love?* Yes, in order that Love be fully satisfied, it is necessary that it lower Itself, and that It lower Itself to nothingness and transform this nothingness into *fire.* . . .[23]

Marie was stunned. In her own sentimental manner she had asked for a note about Jesus' "very sweet" secrets to "His privileged little spouse." This explosion of feeling frightened her. Marie wrote back:

I am seized with a certain sadness at your extraordinary desire for martyrdom. That is indeed the proof of your love. Yes, love you do possess; but not I! ... I fear all that you love. ... I was very close to weeping as I read lines which are not of earth, but an echo from the Heart of God. ... May I tell you? I will: you are possessed by the good God: literally *possessed*, exactly as the wicked are by the devil.[24]

Thérèse wrote back to be sure that Marie did not miss the point. *"Desires"* for Martyrdom meant *"nothing.* ... Jesus said: 'Father, take away this chalice from me.' ... after that how can you say that my desires are the mark of my love? ... what pleases God in my little soul is not that. What pleases Him is *to see me love my littleness and poverty, the blind hope I have in His mercy.* ... He does not say we must look for Him among great souls, but 'afar,' that is in *lowliness, nothingness.* ... Oh! How I wish I could make you realize what I mean! ... It is trust, and nothing but trust, that must bring us to Love. ... Fear brings us only to Justice."[25]

When Thérèse wrote the note to Marie, in the fall of 1896, most of the community did not view her as seriously ill. Her coughing spells had pierced the cloister's silences for so long that the nuns were dulled to them. Sister Teresa of St. Augustine described one episode. "One day during dinner she had a violent fit of coughing. The prioress got tired of listening to her, and said sharply: 'All right, Sister Thérèse, leave us!' "[26]

Besides the prioress, the only nun who knew about the coughing of blood in April was Sister Marie of the Trinity, who thought that Thérèse grew worse after Good Friday. Since Thérèse complained of nothing, Sister Marie tried to intervene. "Unknown to her, I went to Mother Gonzague and asked her to let Sister Thérèse stay in bed during Matins, but she repulsed me, saying, 'I've never seen young people to take such care of their health as you do. There was a time when nobody would be absent from Matins. If Sister Thérèse cannot manage it anymore let her come and tell me so herself.' '"[27] In defense of Mother Gonzague, Thérèse's behavior contrasted sharply with that of most seriously ill patients. She complained of nothing and remained not only cheerful but animated. Despite her poor health she still cherished her dream of exile, and in the fall of 1896 she made one last effort to fulfill that dream. She wanted to leave France to live in a Carmel in Tonkin, present-day Vietnam, where no one knew her.[28] The community prayed for a cure and Mother Gonzague considered sending her, but the dream dissolved in a fit of coughing.[29] Thérèse would not die a martyr in a foreign land. Tucked away in a corner of the town she had lived in since the age of four, she faced not the sword but the cold as the autumn grew damp and the Normandy winter of 1897 began. Each night Thérèse slept in her unheated cell.

Mother Gonzague made one concession to the cold. She gave Thérèse a *chaufferette*, a wooden box with a metal grill for holding hot coals to warm the feet and heat up the alpargatas. Thérèse seldom used it, which annoyed Céline. "Other souls at death," quipped Thérèse, "present themselves before the heavenly court weighted down by their instruments of penance, whereas I shall appear holding up *'ma chaufferette.'* '"[30] During Lent, Thérèse kept the fast — nothing in the morning, meatless soup at 11:00 a.m., and at 6 p.m. six ounces of bread and some fruit, but no hot food.[31] She went off the meatless diet for only one of the six weeks.[32] By April she ran a fever each afternoon, coughed incessantly and was spitting blood. She was ordered to take rest periods in her cell. To loosen her congestion and perhaps combat inflammation, Dr. de Cornière applied the old method of hot plasters, called *vésicatoires*, which blistered the skin.[33]

116

Thérèse's illness brought one unexpected benefit — a renewal of her childhood bond with Pauline. Because Thérèse had been so badly hurt at the loss of her favorite sister, the family believed at first that Pauline was the magnet drawing her into the cloister. Thérèse denied it. Once in the Carmel, she did not seek Pauline's company; she did not confide in Pauline. One did not, Thérèse said, come to the Carmel to live a family life. Yet Thérèse's strong natural feeling for her sister persisted. The two were assigned to work together in the refectory the winter that Louis was hospitalized, but with no chance to chat personally. Pauline even scolded Thérèse for failing to mend a tablecloth on time. The sharp words hurt Thérèse. Later she told Pauline, "You had come to the point where you no longer knew me."[34] Thérèse's feeling flowed into the manuscript that she wrote for Pauline. "It is to you, dear Mother, to you who are doubly my Mother, that I come to confide the story of my soul. . . . It is for *you alone.* . . ."[35] Yet Pauline did not take the time to read these words, and the intimate story that Thérèse spent a year's silences in writing, until two months after Thérèse handed the copybook to her in the choir.

When she finally did read the story, Pauline was astonished at the lines her "little Thérèse" had written. The manuscript powerfully affected her view of her sister. "I said to myself: And this blessed child   is still in our midst! I can speak to her, see her, touch her. Oh! how she is unknown here. And how I am going to appreciate her more now!"[36] Only a year later Thérèse was so ill that Pauline feared she would die. In April and May of 1897 she began making brief visits to her sister. Alone in Thérèse's cell the courtly formality between them crumbled. With Thérèse wasting away from illness, with the Guérins and Léonie outside the walls begging news and her own sense of impending loss, Pauline grasped the most human souvenir at hand — Thérèse's own words. She began to jot down their conversations.[37]

"Does it cause you any pain to pass as a useless member in the minds of the nuns?" Pauline asked.

". . . it makes no difference to me at all."[38]

"Someone told me I shall fear death," Thérèse said a couple of days later. "This could well be true. There isn't anyone here more mistrustful of her feelings than I am."[39] Thérèse told Pauline that when she died she did not want "to be surrounded with wreaths of flowers as Mother Geneviève was."[40]

Thérèse wanted to keep the Rule until she died. Reluctantly, little by little, she had to abandon the daily schedule. On May 18 she was relieved of all duties.[41] On Saturday, May 29, Dr. de Cornière cauterized Thérèse's back for the second time with a treatment called *pointes de feu*,[42] literally points of fire. He punctured her skin several hundred times with hot needles. Céline described how the doctor applied "the cauterizing needle so freely on the wasted body."

> One day I counted more than five hundred applications. As he worked on . . . Thérèse, who had to stand and lean against a table during the process, he conversed with . . . (Mother Gonzague) about the most trivial things. . . . Without waiting for any word of sympathy, . . . (Thérèse) left the room as soon as the treatment was over. Going up to her cell, silent and trembling, she would then sit down on the edge of the wooden plank of her bed, there to endure the long after effects of this drastic treatment.
>
> As yet, she was not considered to be seriously ill. When night came, therefore, she had to sleep on her paillasse. Not having permission to give her a mattress, I could only fold a blanket in four and place it under her sheet.[43]

Seeing the effect of the *pointes de feu* on Thérèse depressed Pauline. The following day Thérèse finally told her sister the truth about her illness — that she had first coughed up blood 14 months earlier.[44] The news shocked and hurt Pauline. Thérèse's illness, she now realized, had been progressing for a very long time. About midnight three days later, Pauline knocked on the door of Mother Gonzague's cell. But she did not come to complain, she did not come to do battle. She came to tell her rival about the manuscript Thérèse had written for her. To still the jealousy, Pauline said, "Now, if you were to order her to do so, she could write something a little more serious, and I am sure it would be much better than the manuscript I have."[45] Thérèse's impending death yanked both women free from pettiness. Mother Gonzague not only agreed to ask Thérèse to write about her life in Carmel for use in an obituary circular to other Carmels, but she granted a remarkable permission. The prioress allowed Pauline to sit privately each day by Thérèse's bedside.[46]

Thérèse began writing her manuscript two days later, on Friday. On Saturday Marie Guérin reported to her father from the Carmel, "She's up and around, but she's experiencing a general state of weakness. She herself now realizes that she's very ill. She feels sharp pains in her side and can eat hardly anything. Yesterday, she threw up her dinner, and frequently in her coughing spells, she vomits. . ."[47] Dr. de Cor*n*ière ordered a milk diet to give Thérèse some strength, and the community prayed for her.[48] Marie Guérin planned to take her picture quickly because she feared that "by the end of the week, her appearance would be so bad, it would be impossible to dream of doing this; especially if Dr. de Corn*i*ère prescribes vesicatories . . . in her weakened state, she'll have trouble recovering from them. . . . Would Mamma please send us some little dishes for her?"[49] Everyone thought she was dying.

But Thérèse rallied, and by mid-June she sat at the bench in her cell or in her father's wheelchair under the chestnut trees and continued to write her thoughts for

Mother Gonzague in a child's copybook. She composed no litany of sweet pious thoughts, nor did she conceal her inner darkness. Thérèse wrote candidly about her trial of faith:

> I must appear to you as a soul filled with consolation and one for whom the veil of faith is almost torn aside; and yet it is no longer a veil for me, it is a wall which reaches right up to the heavens. . . . When I sing of the happiness of heaven and of the eternal possession of God, I feel no joy in this, for I sing simply what I WANT TO BELIEVE . . . at times a very small ray of the sun comes to illumine my darkness, and then the trial ceases for *an instant,* but afterwards the memory of this ray, instead of causing me joy, makes my darkness more dense. . . .(The Lord) did not send me this trial until the moment I was capable of bearing it. A little earlier I believe it would have plunged me into a state of discouragement. Now it is taking away everything that could be a natural satisfaction in my desire for heaven.[50]

Despite the darkness, the doubts, the absence of emotional comfort, Thérèse said she had a greater *"spirit of faith."*[51] Writing spontaneously without corrections Thérèse, though physically weak, now taught Mother Gonzague the essence of Christian charity in clear, strong words. The heart of Christ's message was not to love one's neighbor as oneself. When Jesus spoke of this He said, *"The second commandment is LIKE the first: You shall love your neighbor as yourself."* What He came to teach He summed up the night before He died: *"A new commandment I give you that you love one another: THAT AS I HAVE LOVED YOU, YOU ALSO LOVE ONE ANOTHER."*[52]

. . . How did Jesus love His disciples and why did He love them? Ah! It was not their natural qualities which could have attracted Him . . . they were poor ignorant fisherman . . . still Jesus called them His *friends, His brothers.*[53]

The essence of Christian love became clear to Thérèse as she meditated on Jesus' famous phrase: *"Greater love than this no man has than that he lay down his life for his friends."*

> . . .I understood how imperfect was my love for my Sisters. I saw I didn't love them as God loves them. . . . I understand now that charity consists in bearing with the faults of others, in not being surprised at their weakness, in being edified by the smallest acts of virtue we see them practice. But I understood above all that charity must not remain hidden in the bottom of the heart. . . . *"No one lights a lamp and puts it under a bushel basket, but upon the lampstand, so as to give light to ALL in the house."* It seems to me that this lamp represents charity which must enlighten and rejoice not only those who are dearest to us but "ALL who are in the house," without distinction.[54]

Thérèse based her interpretation not only on the Gospels, which she read almost exclusively toward the end of her life, but on her careful reading of those texts of the Old Testament available to her. She had found the famous "second commandment" in the book of Leviticus:

> When the Lord commanded His people to love their neighbor as themselves, He had not as yet come upon the earth. Knowing the extent to which each one loved himself, He was not able to ask of His creatures a greater love than this for one's neighbor. But when Jesus gave His

Apostles a new commandment, HIS OWN COM-
MANDMENT, as He calls it later on, it is no
longer a question of loving one's neighbor as
oneself but of loving him as *He, Jesus, has
loved him . . . .*[55]
Thérèse found this kind of love for the Sisters she lived
among impossible for her. She could love them only, she
said, if Jesus *"loved them in me."*[56]

Thérèse told Mother Gonzague about Sister Teresa of
St. Augustine — not mentioning her name, but calling her
"a Sister who has the faculty of displeasing me in everything, in her ways, her words, her character; everything
seems *very disagreeable* to me. . . . Not wishing to give
in to the natural antipathy I was experiencing, I told myself that charity must not consist in feelings but in works;
then I set myself to doing for this Sister what I would do
for the person I loved most."[57] Her dislike was so intense
that she "used to run away like a deserter whenever (the)
. . . struggles became too violent." Sister Teresa of St. Augustine was so far from suspecting the truth that one day
she asked her young friend, 'Would you tell me, Sister
Thérèse of the Child Jesus, what attracts you so much toward me? Everytime you look at me, I see you smile.'"[58]

Thérèse was writing in the copybook outside during
haying season.

> . . . at this very moment the infirmarians prac-
> tice in my regard what I have just written; they
> don't hesitate to take two thousand paces when
> twenty would suffice. So I have been able to con-
> template charity in action! Undoubtedly my
> soul is embalmed with it; as far as my mind is
> concerned . . . it is paralyzed in the presence of
> such devotedness. . . . When I begin to take up
> my pen, behold a sister who passes by, a
> pitchfork on her shoulder. She believes she will
> distract me with a little idle chatter: hay,

ducks, hens, visits of the doctor . . . this doesn't last a long time, but there is *more than one good charitable Sister* . . . another hay worker throws flowers on my lap, perhaps believing these will inspire me with poetic thoughts. I am not looking for them at the moment and would prefer to see the flowers remain swaying on their stems. . . . [59]

Thérèse emphasized not "climbing the ladder of perfection," but trust; not the Carmelite Rule, but the command to love one another; not natural feelings but charity, with "its roots (buried) deeply within the soul."[60] At a time when the romantic tradition of the 19th century stamped religious writing with sentimentality, she did not accent "beautiful thoughts" — ". . . if this soul takes delight in her *beautiful thoughts* and says the prayer of the Pharisee, she is like a person dying of hunger at a well-filled table . . . how true it is that God alone knows human hearts and that creatures are terribly narrow in their thoughts!"[61] Nor did she highlight "beautiful prayers." Thérèse wrote of prayer as bluntly as she wrote of her doubts.

Outside the *Divine Office* . . . I do not have the courage to force myself to search out *beautiful* prayers in books. There are so many of them it really gives me a headache! and each prayer is more *beautiful* than the others. . . . I do like children who do not know how to read; I say very simply to God what I wish to say, without composing beautiful sentences, and He always understands me. For me, *prayer* is an aspiration of the heart, it is a simple glance directed to heaven, it is a cry of gratitude and love in the midst of trial as well as joy; finally, it is something great, supernatural, which expands my soul and unites me to Jesus.[62]

Though she loved the prayers said with the community, feeling "that the fervor of my Sisters makes up for my lack of fervor," she disliked repetitious prayers alone. ". . . when alone (I am ashamed to admit it) the recitation of the Rosary is more difficult for me than the wearing of an instrument of penance."[63] She couldn't keep her mind on it. Finally her persistent difficulty in praying was that much of the time she felt no emotional uplift but merely dry, "arid."

The previous May Mother Gonzague had granted Thérèse a spiritual brother, a young man soon to be ordained and sent to the missions, whom Thérèse was to pray for and correspond with. This was Thérèse's second, for Pauline had also assigned her a young priest.[64] Thérèse wrote that she felt responsible for their souls and the souls of her novices but could not bring herself to ask in prayer, as was commonly done, a litany of specific requests for each one. ". . . the days would not be long enough and I fear I would forget something important. For simple souls there must be no complicated ways. . . ." She found the answer to her problem in the phrase from the Canticle of Canticles (Song of Songs 1:4), "*DRAW ME: WE SHALL RUN. . . .*"[65] At this point in the copybook, Thérèse shifts without warning from the detached, slightly playful style in which she addressed Mother Gonzague, to a direct, intimate tone. No longer does she speak to Mother Gonzague but to Jesus. Shedding the language of a servant prostrate and trembling before a master, Thérèse speaks, in her own words, boldly:

> O Jesus, it is not even necessary to say: "*When drawing me, draw the souls whom I love!*" This simple statement, "Draw me," suffices . . . the soul who plunges into the shoreless ocean of Your love draws with her all the treasures she possesses. Lord, You know it, I have no other treasures than the souls it has pleased

You to unite to mine; . . . I dare to borrow the words You addressed to the heavenly Father, the last night which saw You on earth. . . .

"I have glorified you on earth; I have finished the work you gave me to do. And now do you, Father, glorify me with yourself, with the glory I had with you before the world existed. . . .

"I pray for them; not for the world do I pray, but for those whom you have given me, because they are yours; and all things that are mine are yours, and yours are mine; and I am glorified in them. And I am no longer in the world, and I am coming to you. Holy Father, keep in your name those whom you have given to me. . . ." (John 17:4-5, 9-11)

You permitted me to be bold with you. You have said to me as the father of the prodigal son said to his older son: *EVERYTHING that is mine is yours.* Your words, O Jesus, are mine, then, and I can make use of them to draw upon the souls united to me the favors of the heavenly Father. . . . O my Jesus, it is perhaps an illusion but it seems to me that you cannot fill a soul with more love than the love with which you have filled mine. . . . I dare to ask you *"to love those whom you have given me with the love with which you loved me"* . . . here on earth I cannot conceive a greater immensity of love than the one which it has pleased you to give me freely, *without any merit on my part.*

My dear Mother, I finally return to you: I am very much surprised at what I have just written, for I had no intention of doing so.[66]

Writing now in pencil,[67] she closed her manuscript to

Mother Gonzague by writing about the person she imitated most — not Teresa of Avila, the reformer of the Carmelites, but Mary Magdalene. Thérèse liked her style:

> Most of all I imitate the conduct of Magdalene: her astonishing or rather her loving audacity which charms the Heart of Jesus also attracts my own. Yes, I feel it; even though I had on my conscience all the sins that can be committed, I would go, my heart broken with sorrow, and throw myself into Jesus' arms, for I know how much He loves the prodigal child who returns to Him. It is not because God . . . has preserved my soul from mortal sin that I go to Him with confidence and love. . . .[68]

Thérèse never completed the thought. With the words "confidence and love" the sentence and the manuscript abruptly broke off.

It was July. Some days before she wrote these last lines, Thérèse had grown noticeably weaker. After Mass on Friday, July 2nd, Pauline watched as Thérèse made her way painfully from the choir to the oratory. "No one thought of helping her. She walked very quietly close to the wall. I didn't dare offer her my arm."[69]

By now Dr. de Cornière was a presence in the cloister, and his presence set a tone. On Saturday he spoke openly in front of Thérèse about a patient of his who had died, a friend of the Martins. He spoke of their dead friend as an interesting medical case. The woman had died of a tumor. "What a pity," said Dr. de Cornière, "I was unable to make an autopsy." His cold words disturbed Thérèse. "Would he say the same thing," she said to Pauline, "if it were a question of his own mother or sister? Oh! how I would love to leave this sad world!"[70]

Thérèse had had no faith in Dr. de Cornière's "pointes de feu," though she had submitted to the treatment. Clearly she did not have high regard for him. On Wednesday, July 7, Dr. de Cornière witnessed one of her violent attacks of coughing. Later she said to Pauline, "Never shall I forget the scene this morning when I was coughing up blood; Doctor de Cornière had a puzzled look." She even refused Pauline's suggestion that she say "a few edifying and friendly words to Dr. de Cornière."

"Let Dr. de Cornière think what he wants," Thérèse told Pauline. "... I have a horror of 'pretense.' "[71]

During the night Thérèse ran a high fever and her saliva was tinged with blood.[72] The following night, too weak to walk on her own, she was carried to the infirmary — a single room at the end of the ground floor — and placed in Mother Geneviève's bed.[73]

Though a member of the community had died of tuberculosis eight months earlier[1] and Thérèse exhibited classic symptoms, in July 1897 Dr. de Cornière still had not diagnosed the disease. "The news is more and more disturbing," Marie Guérin wrote to her father the day Thérèse was moved to the infirmary.

> Yesterday Dr. de Cornière came twice during the day. He's terribly worried. It's not tuberculosis, but an accident which happened to the lungs, a real lung congestion.
> Yesterday she coughed up blood twice. These are particles of blood that look as if she's vomiting some liver, and all through the remainder of the day, she was coughing up blood. Dr. de Cornière, yesterday morning, forbade her to make any movements; . . . She is constantly taking ice, a drink which is to stop the blood. I think, too, she's being given mustard poultices and mustard under other forms. She had a very bad night . . . her fever was so strong, and, in addition, she was seized with fits of suffocation.[2]

The morning before Marie's letter, when Thérèse vomited blood continually, Dr. de Cornière had watched her with "a puzzled look."[3] Yet as early as 1894 Francis La Néele had treated Thérèse for persistent sore throat, hoarseness and chest pain.[4] The monastery life — sleeping in a room

128

with no heat, rising before dawn and fasting — was very nearly opposite the fresh air, nutritious diet and rest normally recommended for TB. By pronouncing Thérèse healthy the previous summer simply from her outward appearance, Dr. de Cornière had unwittingly pronounced her death sentence.

He was an old-school gentleman. It has been suggested that he tiptoed around the dreaded word tuberculosis as one might today avoid the word cancer.[5] Besides being a feared disease, TB carried with it a social stigma.[6] But it is possible that Dr. de Cornière was simply wrong — that he clung to the discredited fashion among some older French doctors of distinguishing between various chronic lung inflammations and tuberculosis.[7]

Whether the disease that was killing her was called a lung inflammation, tuberculosis or the popular name "consumption" was of no consequence to Thérèse. She was, in her view, being consumed, but not merely in a medical sense. Two years earlier she had prayed to Jesus: ". . . consume Your holocaust with the fire of Your Divine Love."[8] The day before she was carried to the infirmary bed where she would die, Thérèse told Pauline that she had always been fascinated by Job's comment. "Although he should kill me, I will trust in him. . . ."[9]

Thérèse used no words abstractly. Redemption through suffering was as real to her as the face of Christ. "Through his wounds," said Isaiah, "we are healed." Thérèse had shunned the mentality of those who gloried in harsh bodily penances. But the cross was no self-imposed punishment. When in June she wrote the very words that Jesus used to the Father the night before He faced His own death, echoing His plea for "those whom you have given me," Thérèse was not reciting an abstract prayer prostrate before a remote deity. She bonded herself to Christ. She addressed the Father as familiarly as He did. In René Laurentin's phrase, Thérèse "embraced the crucifix not by the feet, but by the face."[10]

As the weeks passed Pauline watched beside Thérèse's bed like thousands of French mothers nursing young victims of TB. But unlike the others who cooled foreheads and changed soaking sheets, Pauline sensed a larger drama unfolding beneath the coughing and the fever and the gasping for breath. The night before they carried Thérèse to the infirmary, Pauline asked her just what had happened when she offered herself to God. "I told you this when it took place," teased Thérèse, "but you paid no attention to me."[11] As the summer wore on, Thérèse said things that made little sense in the context of her anonymous life. Pauline wrote them all down. "I feel especially that my mission is about to begin. My mission of making God loved as I love Him, of giving my little way to souls. . . . I want to spend my heaven in doing good on earth."[12] With nearly a disciple's gaze, she recorded everything: every comment, every line of banter, every small joke that came from her sister's lips. Pauline prodded Thérèse with questions: "What did you do to reach such unchangeable peace?" "I forgot self. . . . I was careful to seek myself in nothing."[13]

But Pauline was no detached observer. She dreaded watching her sister's pain increase, and the air of the infirmary was charged with Pauline's fear. Thérèse chided her. "Why fear in advance? Wait at least for it to happen. . . . I would . . . torment myself by thinking that if persecutions and massacres come . . . someone will perhaps snatch out your eyes!"[14] In the middle of the night of July 19th, Thérèse coughed so violently for a quarter of an hour that she filled a glass with blood.[15] The next day Pauline told her that she feared Thérèse "would suffer death's agonies."[16] Thérèse cut through the vague phrase and brought Pauline back to experience. "If by the agonies of death you mean the awful sufferings which manifest themselves at the last moment through sighs which are frightful to others, I've never seen them here in those who have died under my eyes. Mother Geneviève experienced them in her soul, but not in her body."[17] By that Sunday, Pauline frankly wished her sister would die. Thérèse tried to change the subject. "Are peaches in season? Are they selling plums in the street? I don't know what's happening anymore.

When we reach our declining years we lose both our memory and our head."[18] Marie and Céline were frightened too. Ever the realist, Thérèse saw that her sisters' terror was rooted not merely in their feeling for her, but in their fears for themselves. When Céline cried one day, Thérèse said, "And she really sees that the same thing will happen to her. . . ."[19] The patient cheered the nurses. "With regard to her morale," Marie Guérin wrote on July 10th, "it's always the same: she is gaity itself. . . ."[20] Ringed by gloomy faces and visited regularly by the courtly Dr. de Cornière, Thérèse, a natural mimic, snatched every chance to lighten the mood. She nicknamed the long-haired Dr. de Cornière "Clodion the Hairy" after a Frankish tribal chief.[21] When he pronounced her "better than usual" one day, she clutched her side in mock agony after he'd left. "Yes, yes, she's much better than usual."[22] When the priest refused to give her the sacrament of the dying because she did not appear very sick, Thérèse was piqued. "I sat up in bed out of politeness. I was very pleasant with him. . . . Another time . . . I'll take a cup of milk before his arrival because then I always have a very bad face. I'll hardly answer him, telling him I'm really in agony. Yes, I really see I don't know my business."[23] Again she gripped her side in mock pain. "If you were to see our little patient," Marie Guérin wrote to her father, "you wouldn't be able to stop laughing. . . . There are times when one would pay to be near her."[24]

Besides cheering her sisters with antics, Thérèse began saying tender things to them such as she had not done throughout all her convent life. And she called them by

131

nicknames. "You're my sun,"[25] she told Pauline. Another day, "You have become again for me what you were during my childhood."[26] The distance, the titles vanished. She was dying; they were grieved. Céline became Bobonne. Pauline was simply Mama.[27]

On Friday, July 30th, Marie Guérin wrote to her mother:

> The news is not good ever since yesterday. . . . Dr. de Cornière finds that her sickness has become worse. She's coughing blood every day now, even two and three times a day. It was continuous this morning. She is having chest pains and difficulty in breathing; for minutes she's positively choking. She has to breathe in ether continually, and, at times, her breathing is so bad that the ether has no effect. . . . We see that this cannot last very long. Last night, for example, she had such an intense fever that her back was burning like fire. . . .[28]

The next day Marie wrote her father:

> . . . Yesterday we believed she wouldn't last through the night. Dr. de Cornière feared this too, for when he was here at four o'clock he saw that the blood hadn't stopped since the evening before, and he told Mother Prioress not to wait until tomorrow to give her Extreme Unction.
>
> . . . She is always burning with fever, suffers from chest pains, and a pain in her side.
>
> . . . It's quite impossible to understand her joy at dying. She is like a little child who wants to go with all her heart to see her Father again. . . . She says, "What do you expect? Why should death frighten me? I've never acted except for God." . . . She began . . . talking about everything that would happen at her death . . .

she had us bursting out with peals of laughter. . . . I believe she'll die laughing because she is so happy.[29]

Anticipating the funeral, the nuns carried her *paillasse* down from her cell and hid it in a cell adjoining Thérèse's room. Thérèse caught a glimpse. "Aha!" she cried, "there's . . . (my) paillasse! It's going to be very close to place my corpse on. . . . My little nose was always good!"[30] That week during recreation Sister St. Vincent de Paul wondered aloud why people were speaking of Thérèse as if she were a saint. "She practiced virtue, true, but it wasn't a virtue acquired through humiliations and especially sufferings."[31]

On Sunday, August 1, Thérèse gave Pauline a blunt and strange instruction. In July they had discussed publishing her writings as a vehicle for making known her little way. "After my death," Thérèse now told Pauline, "you mustn't speak to anyone about my manuscript before it is published; you must speak about it only to Mother Prioress." It was, she said, "a very important work," and she foresaw obstacles.[32]

"And I who desired martyrdom," Thérèse said on Wednesday, the 4th of August, "is it possible that I should die in bed?"[33] Thérèse spent that night in agony, with violent pain in her shoulders, right arm and leg, and nightmares. But next morning the coughing of blood had stopped.[34] It was a hot day and Thérèse was exhausted, her mattress soaked through with perspiration.[35] The tall windows were opened onto the cloister green. Thérèse lay in the iron frame bed, the four heavy brown curtains pinched back at the edges. Her sister Marie came in to comfort her after the terrible night and began to utter the sentimental pieties that often filled the sickroom. At Thérèse's death, Marie said, angels would accompany the Lord, "resplendent with light and beauty."

"All these images do me no good," Thérèse said. "I can nourish myself on nothing but the truth. This is why I've never wanted any visions. We can't see, here on earth, heaven, the angels . . . just as they are. I prefer to wait until after my death."[36]

Thérèse's condition had stabilized. The next afternoon as Sister St. Stanislaus, the infirmarian, prepared to go to Vespers, the infirmary was drafty — the door and the window were both open. Thérèse motioned to her to close the door. Sister St. Stanislaus was cheerful, round as an apple and nearly deaf. She didn't close the door but she did fetch a blanket and drape it over Thérèse's feet. Because she was coughing, Thérèse couldn't speak. So the old nun — she was 73 — ambled off and returned with a pillow and another blanket. When Vespers were over about 45 minutes later, Céline found Thérèse bundled up, nearly suffocating under the blankets, and smiling. Mother Gonzague stiffly demanded an explanation, and the scene that followed was scarcely less aggravating than the blankets. Thérèse had to save Sister St. Stanislaus.[37]

On the 8th of August Dr. de Cornière left for a month's vacation, and the Guérins left town for Vichy so Isidore might take the cure for his gout.[38] For the next week Thérèse remained stable, but in the early hours of the morning on Sunday, the 15th, she felt severe pain, this time on her left side. Throughout the next two days she struggled with pain and fever, and by Tuesday she was so weak she could not raise herself up alone.[39] No doctor was called. Francis La Néele, who lived in Caen, was visiting Lisieux and came to the Carmel to see his sister-in-law, Marie Guérin. He asked permission to examine Thérèse.[40] Dr. La Néele finally called the disease that was killing Thérèse by name. Marie Guérin wrote her parents at Vichy. "Francis claimed that for the past week the sickness has made progress in this second lung. He told us that the tuberculosis has reached its last stage. . . ."[41] Nine days later Dr. La Néele himself wrote to Isidore Guérin.

. . . I was moved to tears when I was speaking to her, holding her transparent hands burning with fever. After I examined her, I had her sit up on her pillows. . . . I remained a good half hour with her, along with Céline and Mother Prioress. I kissed her again before I left, and she accompanied me to the door with her smile, which I'll never forget.

The right lung is totally lost, filled with tubercles in the process of softening. The left lung is affected in its lower part. She is very emaciated, but her face still does her honor. She was suffering very much from intercostal neuralgia. . . . I returned there the following Wednesday, hoping to enter once more, but Marie and the little Prioress (Pauline) didn't dare ask Mother Marie de Gonzague's permission for me to do so. I gave her a prescription to calm her pains, for she was suffering very much that day, and I made Céline get permission to see me so as to give her some advice.[42]

By the time Francis La Néele wrote this letter Thérèse had already spent four agonizing days in a new crisis — tuberculosis had invaded her intestines. "You couldn't imagine how bad she is," Marie Guérin wrote her mother on Sunday, August 22nd. "She can no longer do anything by herself. She suffers very much in her joints, and she has continual pain in both her sides. . . . She has intestinal pains, and she can't bear to hear anyone talk or make a move around her. As for her breathing and the fever, they are always the same."[43]

According to Pauline:

She was seized with intestinal pains and her stomach was as hard as a rock. She was no longer able to perform bodily functions except with terrible pains. If we placed her in a seated position to ease the suffocation after a long coughing spell, she thought she was sitting "on iron spikes." She begged prayers because, she said, the pain was enough "to make her lose her reason." She asked that we not leave poisonous medicines within her reach. . . . Besides, she added, if she hadn't any faith, she would not have hesitated for one instant to take her life.[44]

According to Marie, Mother Gonzague refused to summon Dr. La Néele.[45] Thérèse did not want anyone to sit up with her at night.[46] She was alone when the fever was at its worst. "Every morning," Pauline said, "her tongue was dried out so much it looked like a file, a piece of wood."[47]

The following Saturday the family watched and waited. Léonie stayed in the parlor,[48] not permitted to enter the cloister even to see her dying sister. In the infirmary awkward comments filled the silence. Her sisters told Thérèse that the prioress and others were commenting on how pretty she was. ". . . what does that matter to me! It means less than nothing," Thérèse said. "It annoys me. When one is close to death, one can't take any joy out of that."[49] They shifted Thérèse's bed to the center of the infirmary so she could see out the window.[50] "Look! Do you see the black hole . . . where we can see nothing?" she said as she pointed to the clump of chestnut trees. "It's in a similar hole that I am, as far as body and soul are concerned. Ah! what darkness! But I am at peace."[51]

The news of the crisis had brought Madame Guérin back from Vichy. Over the weekend she telegraphed her son-in-law in Caen,[52] and on Monday Dr. La Néele came to Lisieux to see Thérèse. That Thérèse had seen no doctor since his last visit nearly two weeks earlier angered Dr. La Néele, and he spoke bluntly and harshly to the prioress.[53] After he left, Mother Gonzague cried[54] and railed against the Martin clan,[55] but Dr. La Néele had made his point. He was allowed back to see Thérèse twice more before Dr. de Cornière's return on September 10th.[56]

To everyone's surprise Thérèse survived the crisis. Once again she rallied and even grew ravenously hungry. She saw the irony. "I have an appetite that's making up for my whole life. I always ate like a martyr, and now I could devour anything. It seems to me I'm dying of hunger."[57] She craved delicacies. "Since I'm eating now," she told Céline, "I'd really love to have a little chocolate cake, soft inside." Céline suggested a "chocolate patty."

"Oh! no, it's much better; it's long, narrow, I believe it's called an eclair. . . . Only one, however!"[58]

As the slow summer days passed, Thérèse's comments about the truths of the religion she had lived by conveyed sharply what faith did and did not mean to her. Central to the practice of her faith since the age of eleven had been the Eucharist, what she called on the day of her First Communion a "fusion" with Christ. Throughout her life in Carmel Thérèse longed to receive the Eucharist daily, but the prioress disapproved. In mid-August Thérèse faced the agonizing decision to stop receiving Communion. Because of the risk of vomiting, she was given the Eucharist for the last time on August 19th. The next day she sobbed to the point of choking[59] — she would face her death cut off from the sacrament which she viewed as a powerful source of grace. Yet after that day had passed Thérèse did not brood or pine. She dropped the matter completely. Earlier in the summer she had told Pauline, "if you find me dead one morning, don't be grieved. . . Without a doubt it's a great grace to receive the sacraments; but when God doesn't permit it, it's good just the same; everything is grace."[60]

Often the infirmary echoed with the pious comments of visitors — sweet thoughts, sentimental thoughts glowing with feeling but with no link to reality. Just before her crisis in August, Thérèse told Pauline what she thought of

137

the falseness taught in the name of religion, such as the many legends surrounding Jesus, Mary and Joseph. Their lives, she said, were not filled with miracles as in the story of the child Jesus breathing on clay birds to bring them to life. "Everything in their life was done just as in our own."[61] Thérèse was bothered particularly by the romantic legends told about Mary. She wished again that she could have been a priest in order to preach. "One sermon," she said, "would be sufficient."

> We shouldn't say unlikely things or things we don't know anything about! For example, that when she was very little, at the age of three, the Blessed Virgin went up to the Temple to offer herself to God burning with sentiments of love and extraordinary fervor. While perhaps she went there very simply out of obedience to her parents.
>
> Again, why say, with reference to the aged Simeon's prophetic words, that the Blessed Virgin had the Passion of Jesus constantly before her mind from that moment onward? "And a sword will pierce through your soul also," the old man said. It wasn't for the present . . . it was a general prediction for the future. . . .
>
> I must see her real life, not her imagined life. I'm sure her real life was very simple.[62]

Pain and her approaching death did nothing to cloud Thérèse's thinking or relieve her persistent doubts. Her life was drawing to a close in the modern age of discovery, the age of Darwinism and infatuation with the ability of science to uncover immutable truth. Reality, many held, was material, religion outmoded, science limited only by time. The real gains of the scientific method — not the least of which was the discovery of the TB bacillus — could hardly fail to impress one in the habit of judging not

138

from appearance but from experience. The hopes for the triumph of science fanned Thérèse's doubts. "One evening, in the infirmary, she was drawn to confide her troubles to me more than she usually did," Pauline reports. ". . . Up until then, I had known of her trial of faith only vaguely."

"If you only knew what frightful thoughts obsess me," Thérèse told Pauline. "It's the reasoning of the worst materialists . . . making new advances, science will explain everything naturally; we shall have the absolute reason for everything that exists and still remains a problem."[63]

By the popular measuring stick of the day, Thérèse would seem a strange saint. She remained in inner darkness. She had not climbed "the rough stairway of perfection." "I will have the right of doing stupid things up until my death," she told Pauline, "if I am humble and if I remain little."[64] And Thérèse was by no means a disembodied spirit. As her illness became worse she was annoyed by noise, offended by the odor of people's breath and occasionally sharp with Pauline. She cried from the pain, wrestled with doubts and was empty of glowing feelings. In a startling departure from the common practice among the faithful, Thérèse never prayed for a miracle for herself. "Sanctity does not consist in saying beautiful things," she had written to Céline after Louis Martin was placed in the institution, "it does not even consist in thinking them, in feeling them! . . . it consists in *suffering* and suffering *everything*."[65] Now that she *was* suffering everything, Thérèse was empty of self-pity, bitterness and all fear — whether of pain in this life or the next. "Little children," she told Pauline, "are not damned."[66] Her faith was distilled down to enduring the endless pain while trusting God as a dying child still trusts her father.

The respite in early September was brief. On Sunday, September 12th, Thérèse's feet began to swell.[67] "We could not make the least movement around her," Pauline wrote the next day, "such as moving the bed slightly or touching her because it caused her much suffering, so great was her weakness. We were not aware of this at first, and both Sister Marie of the Sacred Heart and I took her pulse for a long period of time. She didn't show any sign of fatigue at first . . . but finally, not being able to stand any more pain, she began to cry. And when we arranged the pillows and her bed cushion, she groaned. . ."[68]

On a visit one September day, Dr. de Cornière chatted with Mother Gonzague in the infirmary about the Carmelites' recent purchase of a lot in the town cemetery. With the cloister cemetery full, the prioress explained, more room was necessary. They intended to dig deeper graves now to accommodate three coffins. "Then it's I who will do first honors to this new cemetery?" quipped Thérèse in front of a startled Dr. de Cornière.

"I already hear one undertaker," Thérèse went on, ". . . 'Don't pull the cord there! Another . . . 'Pull it that way! Hey, be careful! So that's that!' They will throw some earth on my coffin and then everybody will leave."[69]

Talk of Thérèse's burial disturbed Marie. "I understand the thought does something to you," Thérèse told her. "But as for me! What do you want it to do to me? . . . They will place something dead into the ground; it's not as though I were in a trance; then it would be cruel."[70]

On Friday, September 24th, the anniversary of her taking of the veil, Thérèse began her last week alive. The question was not *if* she would die, but on which day. All summer her sisters had speculated about what feast day of the Church Thérèse might die on. Now Pauline asked her if she had any intuitions. "Ah! Mother, intuitions! . . . I know nothing except what you know; I understand nothing except through what I see and feel. . . ."[71]

Thérèse's manner, especially her face, made an impact on the insensitive Dr. de Cornière. "She has the face of an angel," he told Mother Gonzague. "Her face hasn't changed, in spite of her great sufferings. I've never seen

140

that in others before. . . ."[72] The next day, Saturday, Madame Guérin wrote to Jeanne, "Thérèse has spent a very bad night . . . it appears Dr. de Cornière was admiring his patient's gentleness and patience. It seems she's suffering atrociously. He can't understand how she continues to live. . . ."[73]

On Wednesday, September 29, Thérèse could hardly breathe, and the nuns could hear the distinctive sound of a rattle. They gathered around her bedside and recited the prayers for the dying.[74] At one point Thérèse cried, "When shall I be totally suffocated? I can't stand any more!"[75] That night, for the first time in the entire protracted illness, Marie and Céline sat up with her.[76]

In the morning Pauline stayed with Thérèse while the others went to Mass. "She didn't speak a word to me. She was exhausted, gasping for breath; . . . All through the day, without a moment's respite, she remained . . . in veritable torments. She appeared to be at the end of her strength, and nevertheless, to our great surprise, she was able to move, to sit up in her bed."

"You see the strength that I have today!" Thérèse told Pauline. "No, I'm not going to die! I still have strength for months, perhaps years! . . . I no longer believe in death for me. . . . I believe only in suffering. . . ."[77] At one point during the day Marie could barely force herself back into the infirmary. She prayed that her sister would not despair.[78] Everyone who watched Thérèse was moved by her pain, including Dr. de Cornière. During September the doctor suggested injections of morphine. Mother Gonzague would not permit them.[79]

The nuns were summoned back to the room where Thérèse was dying at about 5:00 on Thursday afternoon. According to Pauline:

> When the community entered the infirmary, she welcomed the Sisters with a sweet smile. . . .
> For more than two hours a terrible rattle tore

her chest. Her face was blue, her hands purplish, her feet were cold, and she shook in all her members. Perspiration stood out in enormous drops on her forehead and rolled down her cheeks. Her difficulties in breathing were always increasing, and in order to breathe she made little involuntary cries. All during this time, so full of agony for us, we heard through the window . . . the twittering of robins . . . but this twittering was so strong, so close and so prolonged! I prayed to God to make them keep silent. . . .[80]

For two hours the nuns stayed in the room, praying, watching, waiting. "I left the infirmary," said Sister Marie of the Trinity. "I could no longer bear to assist at so painful a spectacle."[81] Finally, a little past seven, Mother Gonzague sent the nuns away. Thérèse, still alert, was shocked. "Mother! Isn't this the agony! . . ." The prioress assured her it was. As Thérèse looked at the crucifix and said, "I love you," her head fell back on the pillow. The infirmary bell was rung. "Open all the doors," the prioress said, and the sisters flooded into the room and knelt about the bed.[82]

About 20 minutes past seven[83] Thérèse lifted her head again and seemed to look above them. Pauline describes what she saw: "Her face had regained the lily-white complexion it always had in full health; her eyes were fixed above. . . . She made certain beautiful movements with her head. . . . Sister Marie of the Eucharist approached with a candle to get a closer view. . . . There didn't appear any movement in her eyelids. This . . . lasted almost the space of a Credo, and then she gave up her last breath."[84] Sister Mary Magdalene's description: "I saw with amazement how she raised her head again when she seemed to be dead and stared up with a look of amazement and extreme happiness. I have often been present at nuns'

142

deaths, but I have never seen anything like that."[85]

Thérèse was laid out by the grille of the choir[86] for the family and townspeople to view. The following Monday she was buried outside of the cloister in the newly purchased cemetary plot on the hill on the outskirts of town. She was 24 years old.

Leo XIII, the aging pope too deaf to hear her request to enter the cloister nine and one half years earlier, still sat in the papal chair in Rome.

To stop the spread of tuberculosis in the monastery the nuns burned Thérèse's straw bed.[1] Her habit, cape, veils and sandals were to be passed on to someone else but Pauline asked Léonie to offer to buy them back. Mother Gonzague accepted Léonie's offer.[2] Another pair of sandals were too worn to be used. They, too were burned.[3]

Pauline followed Thérèse's instructions about her copybook. Mother Gonzague agreed to publish Thérèse's memories and the letter to Marie in 1896 as well as the pages written for her during June and July on one condition: that the wording be changed to appear as if Thérèse had written everything to her. Pauline agreed to the condition. She copied out the writings and changed the memories Thérèse had written for her and the letter to Marie so that they seemed to be solely for Mother Gonzague.[4] To prevent Mother Gonzague from burning the original copybooks Pauline changed them too.[5]

A month after Thérèse died Mother Gonzague wrote to Godefroy Madelaine, the 55-year-old prior of a Norbertine abbey who had preached the retreat at the Carmel in 1896 and had spoken with Thérèse.[6]

> The recent events here . . . have left me almost lifeless, I don't know whether I'm coming or going. The death of our angel has left me with a void that will never again be filled. The more

aware I become of the perfections of this blessed child, the greater my sorrow at having lost her. Out of obedience, she left me some beautiful pages which I have just taken up again with Mother Agnes of Jesus, and I think we could make them known. This is just for yourself. Would you correct it (the text) for us or, if you are too busy, have it corrected. No one knows about this, not even the community, except the Father Superior[7]. . . .

After editing the pages Father Madelaine gave them to Bishop Hugonin for his approval. "When the bishop heard of a manuscript by Sister Thérèse," Father Madelaine wrote back to Mother Gonzague, "his first reaction was one of distrust of the female imagination."[8] Father Madelaine persuaded the bishop to give his approval. Since the three sections would be published together as a book, a title was needed. The nuns favored *A Canticle of Love* or *The Passing of an Angel*.[9] Father Madelaine suggested taking the title from Thérèse's own first line.

Two thousand copies of *The Story of a Soul* were printed on the first anniversary of Thérèse's death and the book was sent to the French Carmels in place of the customary obituary circular. "It was like a spark," Pauline said. "The Carmels lent the book to people, and requests for it poured in from all sides."[10] Actually, about five books a day were ordered at first, with Pauline filling the orders.[11] In January Father Madelaine wrote to Mother Gonzague, "three days ago in Baycaux one of the most intelligent of the canons told me he had read *The Story of a Soul* three times, and that it gets better each time . . . the students at the major seminary are devouring the dear book."[12] Thérèse had offered her life in Carmel, of course, to save priests.

The Story of a Soul had one major flaw — it was not quite what Thérèse had written. Thérèse had told Pauline to edit her writing and Pauline interpreted these words freely. She corrected spelling, erased, added words and rewrote passages both flattening Thérèse's tone and gilding it with her own flowery style. For example, Pauline dropped Thérèse's bubbling description of Louis on her "wedding day": "Never had he looked more handsome, more *dignified.*" Instead, she inserted: "Advancing towards me, his eyes filled with tears, and pressing me to his heart: '*Ah!*' he cried, '*here is my little queen!*'" Describing a papal blessing, Pauline wrote: "The blessing of the Holy Father, a blessing very precious which will aid me certainly to cross through the raging tempest of my whole life." In addition to adding such passages, Pauline tampered with specific words, replacing "a great sorrow" with "a new unutterable sentiment," and tacking on "weak and mortal" to Thérèse's simple phrase: "this exiled heart."[13] Thérèse filtered out the artificiality, the affectation of style, the sentimentality of her era. Pauline brought it back. As she had decorated the little book she gave Thérèse before her First Communion Pauline now decorated Thérèse's story.

But Thérèse's memory for detail and her freshness cut through Pauline's distortion. No one in the Carmel had imagined the reaction the book unleashed. Pilgrims arrived in Lisieux to visit Thérèse's grave. People wrote to the Carmel reporting cures and a renewed spirit of faith. Five years after *The Story of a Soul* appeared, Pauline, Marie, Céline and Mother Gonzague sat in the Carmel parlor and listened to the idea of Father Thomas Taylor, a Scottish priest born the same year as Thérèse and ordained the year she died, that Thérèse be canonized.[14] Mother Gonzague laughed, "In that case how many Carmelites would it be necessary to canonize?"[15] Isidore Guérin would have nothing to do with an effort to have his niece declared a saint.

By 1905, eight years after Thérèse's death, *The Story of a Soul* had been translated into English, Polish, Italian,

Spanish, Dutch, Portuguese, German, Japanese and Russian.[16] The letters kept coming and so did the pilgrims, many of them priests. And so did young women eager to be Carmelites like Thérèse. They came from France, Ireland, Italy, Portugal, even Istanbul — too many for the small monastery to hold.[17] One of these new nuns, Mother Marie-Ange of the Child Jesus — started the official steps toward canonization.[18] Isidore Guérin and another formidable opponent — the bishop of Bayeaux — dropped their objections[19] and by 1909 the way was clear.

The public may have been calling Thérèse a saint, but the Church was not. Gone were the days when someone was swiftly, sometimes carelessly, proclaimed a saint. In modern times the Church moved slowly — Canon Law required 50 years before the official discussion of the heroism and virtue of a prospective saint.[20] But by 1909 the Carmel was receiving 50 letters a day from all parts of the world[21] with many reports of cures and the transforming of lives. In a remarkable move a diocesan tribunal opened preliminary hearings in Lisieux in the summer of 1910, just 13 years after Thérèse died. The primary focus was not Thérèse's writings or theology, or even the claims of cures after her death, but Thérèse herself. They wanted to know what people remembered about her, what they knew firsthand. By starting the tribunal so soon after her death, the investigators gained the relatively fresh testimony of people who had known Thérèse. Listening to the memories of the 48 witnesses took the tribunal over a year.[22]

Everyone who knew Thérèse had a chance to tell what he or she remembered: Sister Teresa of St. Augustine, the nun appearing in *The Story of a Soul* as a source of struggle to Thérèse because of her natural revulsion; Sister Martha of Jesus, who had served Thérèse tainted food; and Sister Aimée of Jesus, who resented the pyramid of Martin girls in the Carmel and opposed Céline's entry. "I was one of the instruments God made use of to sanctify her," Sister Aimée testified. "The charitable way she bore with my defects brought her to an outstanding degree of holiness."[23] Neither Mother Gonzague nor Marie Guérin was there. The prioress had died in 1904 of cancer of the tongue, and Thérèse's cousin Marie had died the following year of tuberculosis.[24]

The testimony revealed both the tidal wave of reaction to Thérèse and its impact on the quiet Carmel. "I was given the job of preparing little pictures," testified Sister Martha of Jesus, "to which we then attached little souvenirs. . . . I prepared 23,000 of them in one year and they were not enough to satisfy the demand."[25] Sister Marie of the Trinity said, "I am amazed by the volume of mail received here every day; it comes from all over the world. . . . At the moment we are getting an average of 100 letters a day."[26] Pauline, once again the prioress, kept careful accounts. From July 1909 to July 1910 the community had received 36,612 requests for souvenirs and 183,348 requests for pictures of Thérèse.[27]

A few weeks after the tribunal opened, Thérèse's body was taken from its plain grave and placed in a cement vault. The wooden cross that had marked her grave was taken to the Carmel. Every bit of the cross, Céline told the investigators, was carved with requests or thanks.[28]

With thousands of people clamoring to know Thérèse, the Martin sisters had had to decide what sort of Thérèse to make known. Much of what people asked struck them as too intimate. Their own feelings toward their dead sister were understandably tender and protective. As Thérèse's fame spread, people especially wanted to know what this "saintly" nun looked like. Due to Céline's taking her camera into the cloister with her, Thérèse had been photographed.

However, to Céline the word saint evoked not photographs, but romantic religious art — luminous faces of celestial beauty. Just as Pauline had dressed up Thérèse's memories, Céline began to retouch the photographs she herself had taken. Still disatisfied, she decided to paint a

148

portrait of Thérèse, a portrait less concerned with the details of her features than with radiating saintliness. "In her sleep of death, on Thérèse's countenance there was a reflection of eternal happiness and a celestial smile," Céline later wrote.

That which struck me most, however, was a certain vitality and joy with which her eyelids (tightly closed) seemed to vibrate. Death was forgotten while this consolation lasted. I might add that in all my contacts with our Sisters who have died since then, I have never noticed anything like it.

Since Thérèse was so beautiful in death, I tried to take her picture before she was carried from the infirmary to the choir on October 1, 1897, . . . I was not very successful, although her heavenly smile did come through. . .

I took another photograph on Sunday, October 3, in the afternoon while she lay exposed on a flowery bier in the choir. But this picture showed her features to be elongated, and curiously, her blond eyebrows were dark brown — almost black. She was still majestic, but we could no longer recognize her.

It was for this reason that, in 1905, at the urgent request of the community, I painted a picture of Thérèse as she had appeared immediately after death. For model, I used the first picture taken in the infirmary on October 1, 1897. The sisters who had been her contemporaries considered my portrait a perfect likeness of our Saint. It was this picture which was published in all editions of *Histoire d'Une Ame* (*Story of a Soul*) after the year 1906.[29]

It is unlikely that Céline intentionally distorted her sister. Undoubtedly her photographs failed to convey all that she saw in Thérèse. But Céline was also in the grip of a fixed idea. She thought art a higher expression of truth than photography, and she thought herself an artist.[30] A letter that Canon Dubosq, an official in the beatification process, wrote to her in 1911 reflects Céline's point of view:

> Our ideas and our tastes are in absolute agreement regarding the photographic question. There are many who say that photography, because it acts mechanically, is a witness to pure truth, while the work of the artist must be suspected of fantasy and caprice because of the artist's own activity. Well, I believe just the opposite. Very often it is the photograph which is false, while the artist, if he be sensitive and honest, can make his subject live. He can study, feel, observe sentiments and affections, indeed, the very character of his subject; then he gathers these fleeting and most indicative expressions of the face which best reflect the soul of his subject.[31]

As Father François de Sainte-Marie has said, "Canon Dubosq's reasoning is valid, provided the artist is a great one."[32] Céline was not.

The sisters in the community may have thought her portrait a perfect likeness, but Léonie, Isidore Guérin and Jeanne and Francis La Néele did not. In 1913 Céline wrote Léonie, "Francis came to the parlor on business the other day, and he scolded all of us, especially me, claiming that none of my portraits resembled Thérèse."[33] With copies of the portraits being sent all over the world in place of the photographs, the La Néeles had a photograph of Thérèse reproduced and circulated on their own.[34] Though the early portrait of Thérèse drawn from a picture taken in 1895 did,

150

in fact, resemble her, as time passed and the real Thérèse grew ever more distant, Céline's portraits became more fanciful. She added roses, heavenly rays of light, and idealized Thérèse's features. She also painted scenes from her sister's childhood. Céline's brush created the image of Thérèse the world came to know as the "Little Flower."

The 1910 tribunal was only a preliminary hearing to determine whether the Church should proceed. The official Apostolic Process opened in 1915. By this time *The Story of a Soul* had been translated into 35 languages and the Carmel had sent out over eight million pictures of Thérèse.[35] After 91 sessions and two and a half years the investigation was closed. By 1919, when the Carmel was receiving over 500 letters a day, Cardinal Vico, prefect of the Congregation of Rites, quipped, "We have to hurry up and glorify the little saint if we don't want the voice of the people to outrun us."[36] There were no doubts about Thérèse herself, but to declare her a saint the Church had to undertake one more investigation — that of claimed miracles.

Ever since 1899, hundreds of letters to the Carmel had reported spontaneous cures after visiting Thérèse's grave or praying to her or touching something of hers — a petal of a flower or a fragment of her cloak. This letter was dated April 3, 1911: "M. was attacked in 1909 with pains in the lumbar region, which lasted three months and which had not completely disappeared when a relapse took place at the end of December 1910. The pains, which resisted all treatment and forced the sick child to keep her bed, disappeared suddenly the 29th of March, at 3 p.m., on the termination of a novena made by all the personnel of the establishment (an orphanage) to Soeur Thérèse." The statement was signed by the doctor whose injections, cauterizations and electrical treatments had failed to relieve the child's "intolerable" suffering. "All the joints of the vertebrae column were diseased, but especially the lower part, where the least touch made her shudder." At 3

151

o'clock on March 29 the child heard a sound in the next room, jumped out of bed to see what it was and, finding her pain was gone, rushed downstairs.[37]

Many more letters told of a powerful new inner life wiping away years of anxiety: a French girl tormented by scruples; an old man frightened for years that he would be damned; a young priest who suffered from constant depression. Letters poured in from all over — Italy, Canada, Australia, Hungary, Uganda, the Solomon Islands.[38]

The stories of cures were often moving, certainly sincere, but how accurate were the diagnoses? Were other explanations possible? Because the cures were not validated, the Church did not officially approve them. To give its approval the Church required an investigation which eliminated all natural explanations for the cure. It also required a written diagnosis by respected physicians dated before the return of health and based on scientific techniques such as x-rays. The inquiry into claimed cures began in 1922 — only after all investigations of Thérèse herself were concluded — and was limited to four cases.

In 1923 the Church approved of two spontaneous cures unexplained by medical treatment: Sister Louise of St. Germain, who suffered stomach ulcers between 1913 and 1916, and the very recent case of Charles Anne, a 23-year-old seminarian who was dying from advanced pulmonary tuberculosis. The night he thought he was dying, Charles Anne prayed to Thérèse. Afterward, the examining doctor testified, "The destroyed and ravaged lungs had been replaced by new lungs, carrying out their normal functions and about to revive the entire organism. A slight emaciation persists, which will disappear within a few days under a regularly assimilated diet."[39] Thérèse was beatified — the step just before canonization.

In 1925 two more cures were approved: Gabrielle Trimusi from Parma, Italy, who suffered from arthritis of the knee and tubercular lesions on the vertebrae,[40] and Maria Pellemans of Schaerbeck, Belgium, who suffered

from pulmonary tuberculosis which had spread, as Thérèse's illness had, to the intestines. The diagnosis of
pulmonary and intestinal tuberculosis was made by a Dr.
Vandensteene, who also examined Maria after she came
back from visiting Thérèse's grave. The doctor testified,
"I found Miss Pellemans literally transformed. This
young woman, out of breath from the least movement,
moves about without fatigue; she eats everything given to
her, with a very good appetite. The abdomen presents no
tender point, when formerly the least pressure produced
severe pain. All symptoms of tubercular ulceration of the
intestine have disappeared."[41] In reports predating
Maria's return to health, two other physicians confirmed
Dr. Vandensteene's diagnosis of pulmonary and intestinal
tuberculosis.[42]

Thérèse was declared a saint on May 17, 1925, five
years and one day after Joan of Arc, but the celebration
for Thérèse far outshone that for the famous heroine of
France. Pope Pius XI decided to revive the old custom of
outlining St. Peter's with torches and lamps. Ropes, lamps
and tallows were pulled from the dusty storerooms where
they had been packed away for 55 years. A few old work-
men who remembered how it was done the last time — in
1870 — directed 300 men for two weeks as they climbed
about fastening lamps to St. Peter's dome.[43]

The day of the ceremony the scene in Rome bore little
resemblance to the day when Father Révérony and the
Swiss Guards had pried Thérèse away from Pope Leo
XIII's knees. "All Rome Admires St. Peter's Aglow for a
New Saint," read the headline of *The New York Times'*
front-page story.

Well over 60,000 persons, probably the largest
crowd that ever had been inside St. Peter's Basilica at any one time since the coronation of
Pius X, 22 years ago, watched the Pope begin today a series of jubilee year canonizations . . .

by raising to sainthood the French nun Sister Thérèse of the Infant Jesus.

... (The pope) was dressed in full Pontifical robes. ... He was followed by all the Cardinals present in Rome ... and by a group of over 200 Bishops and Archbishops from every part of the world. ...[44]

People had begun to enter the dark basilica at 4:00 in the morning. By 6:00 a.m., two hours before the start of the ceremony, St. Peter's was filled. Departing from tradition, the Pope used a loudspeaker for the first time in St. Peter's so that every person there heard him proclaim Thérèse Martin a saint. Outside, the news was conveyed to the thousands jamming the square by the blare of silver bugles from St. Peter's dome and the ringing of the bells of Rome's 400 churches.

At nightfall, the 300 workers again clambered up the dome to light the hundreds of lamps. St. Peter's was blazing, said *The Times'* correspondent, "like a huge torch." The square, which held 200,000, was overflowing. People climbed onto every rooftop and drove to every hill inside and outside of Rome from which they might glimpse the spectacle. About a million people saw the lighted dome.[45]

As theologians, philosophers, artists turned their attention to Thérèse it became clearer that the implications of her little way of trust and confidence were not so little at all. She was truly a *modern* saint. To Henri Bergson she represented the spiritual *élan* at the heart of his philosophy, over against "the closed religion." In his view Thérèse Martin was a greater saint than Teresa of Avila.[46] The French writer Georges Bernanos kept a copy of Thérèse's last conversations at his bedside[47] and modeled after her the young priest in his *Diary of a Country Priest*. He, like Thérèse, dies without the Sacrament of the Eucharist. His last words come directly from her: "everything is grace."[47] Thomas Merton said Thérèse

154

was responsible for his final decision to enter the Trappists. And Maximilian Kolbe, the Polish priest who took the place of a prisoner condemned to starve to death at Auschwitz, and who was recently named a saint, made a pilgrimage to Lisieux.

Inevitably St. Thérèse in a golden halo was stamped on thousands of dishes and trays and bright plastic statues. It was an irony. "We should never make any false currency in order to redeem souls,"[48] Thérèse had told Pauline the day she was finally carried down to the infirmary to die. The garish marketing of "the little rose-water saint" outraged those who had known the real Thérèse. But Thérèse was not the saint merely of those with refined tastes, but of millions of ordinary people.

Marie, Pauline, Léonie and Céline Martin all lived to see their sister canonized a saint. Marie died in 1940, Léonie in 1941, Pauline in 1951. In 1959 Céline, the last of the Martin family, died in the Carmel of Lisieux.

Sources

Arminjon, Charles. *Fin du Monde Présent et Mystères de la Vie Future* (1881). Lisieux: Office Central, 1970.

Beevers, John L. *St. Thérèse of Lisieux: The Making of a Saint*, Rockford, Ill.: Tan, 1976.

Carmel de Lisieux. *Le Centenaire de la Fondation du Carmel de Lisieux, 1838-1938*. Lisieux: Carmel, 1938.

Clarke, Hugh, O. Carm., and Edwards, Bede, O.D.C., General Editors. *The Rule of Saint Albert*. London: Carmelite Book Service, 1973.

Clarke, John. O.C.D. Trans. *St. Thérèse of Lisieux, Her Last Conversations*. Washington: Institute of Carmelite Studies, 1977. (Translation of *J'Entre Dans La Vie, Derniers Entretiens*. Paris: Cerf-Desclée de Brouwer, 1973.)

Clendening, Logan. *Source Book of Medical History*. New York: Dover Publications, Inc., 1960.

De Meester, Conrad. *Dynamique de la Confiance: Genèse et structure de la "voie d'enfance spirituelle" chez Ste. Thérèse de Lisieux*. Paris: Les Éditions du Cerf, 1969.

Dubos, René and Jean. *The White Plague, Tuberculosis, Man and Society*. Boston: Little, Brown and Company, 1952.

Gaucher, Guy. *Histoire d'Une Vie*. Paris: Cerf, 1982.

——————. *La Passion de Thérèse de Lisieux, 4 Avril — 30 Septembre, 1897*. Paris: Cerf-Desclée de Brouwer, 1973.

Laurentin, René. *Thérèse de Lisieux, Mythes et Réalité*. Paris: Beauchesne, 1972.

Martin, Céline (Sister Geneviève of the Holy Face). *A Memoir of My Sister St. Thérèse*. New York: P.J. Kenedy & Sons, 1959.

Martin, Thérèse. *Collected Letters of Saint Thérèse of Lisieux*. Ed. Abbé Combes. trans. F.J. Sheed. New York: Sheed and Ward, 1949.

——————. *Derniers Entretiens*. Paris: Cerf-Desclée de Brouwer, 1971.

——————. *St. Thérèse of Lisieux, General Correspondence*, vol. 1, 1877-1890. Trans. John Clarke, O.C.D. Washington: Institute of Carmelite Studies, 1982. (Translation of *Correspondance Générale I*, Paris: Cerf-Desclée de Brouwer, 1972.)

Histoire d'Une Ame, Lisieux: Office Central de Lisieux, 1949.

Manuscrits autobiographiques, François de Sainte-Marie, O.C.D., Trans., Lisieux: Carmel, 1957.

——————. *Story of a Soul*. John Clarke, O.C.D., trans. Washington; Institute of Carmelite Studies, 1976. (Translation of *Histoire d'Une Ame, Manuscrits autobiographiques*, Paris: Cerf, Desclée de Brouwer, 1972.)

Martin, Zélie. *Correspondance familiale, 1863-1877*. Lisieux: Office Central, 1958.

Mettler, Cecilia. *History of Medicine*. Philadelphia: The Blakiston Company, 1947.

O'Mahoney, Christopher, O.C.D., Ed. and trans. *St. Thérèse of Lisieux by those who knew her*. Huntington, Indiana: Our Sunday Visitor, 1975.

Piat, Stéphane-Joseph, O.F.M. *Sainte Thérèse de Lisieux à la découverte de la voie d'enfance*. Paris: Editions franciscaines, 1964.

Rohrback, Peter-Thomas, O.C.D., trans. *Photo Album of St. Thérèse of Lisieux.* New York: P.J. Kenedy and Sons, 1962 (Translation of *Visage de Thérèse de Lisieux,* Lisieux: Office Central).

Sackville-West, Victoria Mary. *The Eagle and the Dove.* London: Michael Joseph, 1953.

Saint John of the Cross. *Ascent of Mount Carmel.* Third Revised Edition. Trans. and ed. E. Allison Peers. Garden City, New York: Image Books (Doubleday), 1958.

——————. *The Dark Night of the Soul,* Trans. David Lewis, London: Thomas Baker, MCMVIII.

——————. *Living Flame of Love.* Trans. and ed. E. Allison Peers. Garden City, New York: Image Books (Doubleday), 1962.

Saint-Léon, Mère. *La Petite Thérèse à L'Abbaye.* Lisieux: Notre Dame du Pré, 1930.

Serrou, Robert, and Vals, Pierre. *Le Carmel: Carmelites et Carmes.* Paris: Editions Pierre Horay, 1957.

Six, Jean-François. *La Veritable Enfance de Thérèse de Lisieux, Nervrose et Sainteté.* Paris: Editions du Seuil, 1971, and *Thérèse de Lisieux au Carmel,* Paris: Editions du Seuil, 1973.

Summarium. A summary of the process of beatification and canonization of Sister Thérèse of the Child Jesus. 1916, 1920. On file in the Archives of the Carmel of Lisieux.

Thomas à Kempis. *Of the Imitation of Christ.* London: Methuen & Co., 1905.

Abbreviations of major sources

AMC	*Ascent of Mount Carmel*
CF	*Correspondance familiale, 1863-1877*
CL	*Collected Letters of St. Thérèse of Lisieux*
DE	*Derniers Entretiens*
DN	*Dark Night of the Soul*
GC	*Saint Thérèse of Lisieux: General Correspondence. Volume 1, 1877-1890*
IC	*Of the Imitation of Christ*
LA	*St. Thérèse of Lisieux, her last conversations*
LC	Letters to Thérèse in *General Correspondence*
LD	Diverse letters among Thérèse's correspondents in *General Correspondence*
LFL	*Living Flame of Love*
LT	Letters from Thérèse in *General Correspondence*
ME	Céline Martin (Geneviève of St. Thérèse) *A Memoir of My Sister St. Thérèse*
Ms. A	Autobiographical manuscript dedicated to Pauline Martin, 1895, in *Story of A Soul*
Ms. B	Letter to Marie Martin, September, 1896 in *Story of a Soul*
Ms. C	Autobiographical manuscript dedicated to Mother Marie de Gonzague, 1897 in *Story of A Soul*
SU	Summarium
TE	*St. Thérèse of Lisieux by those who knew her: Testimonies from the process of beatification*

Chapter notes

CHAPTER 1 — Introduction

1 Quoted in Peter-Thomas Rohrback, O.C.D., *Photo Album of St. Thérèse of Lisieux*, New York, 1962, p. 22.

2 Guy Gaucher, *Histoire d'Une Vie*, Paris, 1982, p. 103.

3 Ms. A, p. 139.

4 She straightened her handwriting in 1894. René Laurentin, *Thérèse de Lisieux, Mythes et Réalité*, pp. 211, 212.

5 Quoted in Rohrback, p. 22.

6 Ms. A, p. 108

7 Laurentin, p. 207

8 Ms. A, p. 108

9 Msgr. Durand, *The Lisieux Guide for Pilgrims and Visitors*, p. 5.

10 Ibid., p. 15.

11 Ms. A, p. 74.

12 Quoted by Ernest J. Simmons in the Foreword to Ann Dunnigan, Trans., *Anton Chekhov: Selected Stories* (New York: New American Library, 1960), p. XIV.

158

CHAPTER 2 — The Martins

1 Zélie to Madame Guérin, Jan. 3, 1873. CF, p. 141.

2 GC, p. 104; see also n. 5, (quoted from testimony of Louise Marais, July 22, 1923).

3 Zélie to Isidore, July 14, 1864. CF, p. 24.

4 Guy Gaucher, *Histoire d'Une Vie* (Paris, 1982), p. 12.

5 Zélie to Isidore, April 23, 1865. CF, pp. 28-30.

6 Zélie to Isidore, Nov. 7, 1865. CF, p. 34.

7 Zélie to Isidore, March 5, 1865. CF, p. 27.

8 Zélie to Isidore, Aug. 24, 1868. CF, p. 64.

9 Zélie to the Guérins, Aug. 29, 1869. CF, p. 81.

10 Zélie to the Guérins, Feb. 24, 1870. CF, pp. 87-89

11 Zélie to Isidore, Oct. 1870. CF, p. 102.

12 Ibid., pp. 102-103.

13 Zélie to Isidore, Jan. 17, 1873. CF, p. 144

14 Zélie to Madame Guérin, March 1873. CF, p. 149.

15 Ibid., pp. 149-50.

16 Zélie to Pauline, May 22, 1873. CF, p. 170.

17 Ms. A, pp. 21-22.

18 Zélie to Madame Guérin, July 20, 1873. CF, p. 176.

19 Zélie to Isidore, March 29, 1874. CF, p. 194.

20 Ms. A, p. 22.

21 Ms. A, pp. 23-24.

22 Zélie to Madame Guérin, Nov. 12, 1876. CF, p. 323.

23 Zélie to Louis, Dec. 24, 1876. CF, p. 336.

24 Gaucher, *Histoire d'Une Vie*, pp. 11-13, and Jean-Francois Six, *La Veritable Enfance de Thérèse de Lisieux* (Paris, 1971), pp. 51-52.

25 Zélie to Madame Guérin, Dec. 17, 1876. CF, p. 333.

26 Ms. A, p. 28.

27 Ms. A, p. 33.

28 Ms. A, p. 33-34.

29 LD, From Isidore Guérin to Louis Martin, Sept. 10, 1877, GC, pp. 127-128.

30 Ibid.

31 Six, *La Veritable Enfance de Thérèse de Lisieux*, pp. 161-167.

32 GC, p. 119 and 123.

33 Gaucher, *Histoire d'Une Vie*, p. 30.

34 Ms. A, p. 43.

35 Ms. A, p. 42.

36 Six, p. 175.

37 For a description of Lisieux in 1870s see GC, p. 122 (quoted from Levasseur, *Geographie du departement du Calvados*, Caen, 1874).

38 Ms. A, p. 37.

39 Ms. A, p. 48.

40 Ms. A, pp. 45-46.

41 Ms. A, p. 46.

42 Ms. A, p. 36.

43 Ms. A, p. 44.

44 Testimony of Sr. Agnes of Jesus, TE, p. 38.

45 Ms. A, pp. 40-41.

46 Ms. A, p. 53.

47 The attitude of the nuns and of the other students toward Thérèse was described by a member of the Benedictine Sisters of Notre Dame-du-Pré, Lisieux, in an interview on July 22, 1983. Name withheld on request.

48 Ms. A, p. 87.

49 Ms. A, p. 54.

50 Ms. A, p. 57.

51 Ms. A, p. 58.

52 Ms. A, pp. 59-60

53 GC, p. 151, n. 2 (Sister Marie of the Sacred Heart in *Souvenirs autobiographiques*, p. 74.)

54 Ms. A, p. 60.

55 Ms. A, p. 60-61

56 GC, p. 162 (Quoted from Apostolic Process, 1915-1916, Vol. 2 of the Summary).
57 Testimony of Sr. Marie of the Sacred Heart, TE, p. 86.
58 Testimony of Sr. Marie of the Sacred Heart, GC, p. 162. (Quoted from Preparatory Notes for the Bishop's Process, 1908, p. 4.)
59 Ms. A, p. 62.
60 Testimony of Sr. Marie of the Sacred Heart, TE, p. 87.
61 Testimony of Jeanne Guérin, TE, p. 268, and GC, p. 162.
62 Testimony of Sr. Marie of the Sacred Heart, TE, p. 87.
63 Ms. A, p. 64, and Gaucher, *Histoire d'Une Vie*, p. 49.
64 Ms. A, p. 61.
65 Testimony of Sr. Marie of the Sacred Heart, GC, p. 162. (Quoted from Preparatory Notes from the Bishop's Process, 1908, p. 5.)
66 Ms. A, p. 62-63.
67 Pauline to Thérèse, LC 10, around April 2, 1883, GC, p. 163.
68 Ibid.
69 Pauline to Thérèse, LC 12, beginning of May, 1883 (approximate date). GC, p. 169.
70 Ms. A, p. 65, and Testimony of Sr. Marie of the Sacred Heart, TE, p. 87.
71 Ms. A, p. 67.
72 Ibid.
73 It was customary to receive First Communion at the age of 10. The previous year Thérèse had missed the cut-off date, Jan. 1, by one day.
74 Ms. A, p. 74.
75 Ms. A, p. 81.
76 Pauline to Thérèse, LC 7, end of Dec. 1882 or Jan. 1883, GC p. 157.
77 Pauline to Thérèse, LC 26, March 13, 1884, GC, p. 193.

78 Testimony of Agnes of Jesus, TE, p. 24, and GC, p. 191, footnote 4.
79 Ms. A, p. 77.
80 Ms. A, p. 78.
81 Ms. A, p. 76.
82 Six, *La Veritable Enfance de Thérèse de Lisieux*, p. 201. (Thérèse's retreat notes, quoted from P. François de Sainte-Marie: *Notes et Tables*, pp. 22-27).
83 Ms. A, p. 84.
84 See Letter from Thérèse to Marie Guérin, LT 92, May 30, 1889. GC, p. 567-568.
85 Ms. A, p. 88.
86 Six, *La Veritable Enfance de Thérèse de Lisieux, p. 210.*
87 *Ibid.*
88 *Ms. A, p. 88.*
89 *Gaucher, Histoire d'Une Vie*, p. 60.
90 Thérèse mentions "several lessons a week" in Ms. A, p. 85, but according to invoices cited in GC, p. 242, n. 1, Thérèse was tutored at first four and later eight times a month, for one hour.
91 Ms. A, p. 85.
92 Ms. A, p. 90.
93 GC, pp. 212-215, and Ms. A, p. 89.
94 Ms. A, p. 90.
95 Ms. A, 82.
96 Ms. A, p. 48.
97 Ms. A, pp. 90-91.
98 Ms. A, p. 91.
99 Ms. A, p. 92.
100 Letter from Marie To Thérèse, LC 46, Nov. 1886, GC, p. 254.
101 Gaucher, *Histoire d'Une Vie*, p. 64.
102 Ms. A, p. 101.
103 Ms. A, p. 98.
104 Ibid.
105 Ibid.

CHAPTER 3 — The Campaign

1 IC, Book II, Chapter 1, p. 33.
2 IC, Book II, Chapter 1, p. 34.
3 IC, Book II, Chapter 1, p. 33.
4 Ms. A, 101.

5 l'Abbé Arminjon, *Fin du Monde Présent et Mystéres de la View Future.* (1881) (Reprinted Lisieux, Office Central, 1970) pp. 291-292, 297.

6 Ms. A, p. 102.

7 Ms. A, p. 87.

8 Ms. A, p. 104.

9 Ms. A, p. 103.

10 Ms. A, p. 104.

11 Ms. A, p. 105 (quoted from John of the Cross, see n. 110).

12 Ms. A, p. 106.

13 According to the translation of Christopher O'Mahoney, O.C.D., Pauline Martin, in her testimony at the process of beatification, referred to Mother Marie de Gonzague as Mother Gonzague. This abbreviated version of the prioress's name has been adopted here.

14 Ms. A, p. 59.

15 Mother Marie de Gonzague to Thérèse, LC 6, end of Dec. 1882 or Jan. 1883. GC, pp. 155-156.

16 GC, p. 262, (quote from the testimony of P. Godefroy Madelaine, The Bishop's Process, 1910-1911, p. 131).

17 GC, p. 252, n. 6 (quote from Sister Marie of the Sacred Heart, Souvenirs autobiographiques, p. 76).

18 Ms. A, p. 108.

19 Six, La Veritable Enfance de Thérèse de Lisieux, pp. 232-232.

20 Ibid.

21 Ms. A, p. 100.

22 GC, p. 290, n. 2.

23 Thérèse to Pauline, LT 27, Oct. 8, 1887, GC, 288.

24 Ms. A, p. 109.

25 Thérèse to Pauline, LT 27, Oct. 8, 1887, GC, p. 289.

26 Pauline to Isidore Guérin, LD Oct. 21, 1887. GC, pp. 295-6.

27 Ms. A, p. 110 and GC, p. 207, n. 4.

28 Incident described in a letter from Céline Martin to the prioress of Notre Dame du Pré, Nov. 19, 1949.

29 Ms. A, p. 111.

30 Ms. A, p. 115.

31 Ms. A, p. 116.

32 Ms. A, pp. 116-117.

33 Ms. A, p. 117.

34 Céline to Pauline and Marie, LD, Nov. 5-6, 1887, GC, p. 305.

35 Thérèse to Pauline and Marie, LT 30, Nov. 6, 1887, GC, p. 308.

36 Ms. A, p. 72.

37 Ms. A, p. 130.

38 Ms. A, p. 131.

39 Ms. A, p. 140.

40 Ibid.

41 Pauline to Thérèse, LC 59, Nov. 10, 1887, GC, p. 315.

42 Ms. A, p. 132.

43 GC, p. 339, n. 5 (quoted from Fueillet, Péleringage de Rome, printed at Coutances).

44 Ms. A, p. 134.

45 For another point of view on Abbé Révérony's comment see GC, p. 352, n. 2.

46 Ms. A, p. 134.

47 Ibid.

48 Ms. A, p. 134-135.

49 Thérèse to Pauline, LT 36, Nov. 20, 1887, GC, p. 353.

50 GC, p. 376, (quoted from Nov. 24 issue of L'Univers).

51 Pauline to Céline, LD, Nov. 26, 1887, GC, p. 372.

52 Pauline to Louis Martin, LD, Nov. 25, 1887, GC, p. 368.

53 Pauline to Isidore Guérin, LD, Nov. 28-29, 1887, GC, p. 376.

54 Ibid.

55 Pauline to Céline, LD, Nov. 26, 1887, GC, p. 372.

56 Céline to Pauline and Marie, LD, Nov. 23, 1887 GC, p. 356.

57 Céline to Pauline and Marie, LD, Nov. 28, 1887, p. 374.

58 Ms. A, p. 139.

59 Celine to Pauline and Marie, LD, Nov. 29, 1887, GC, p. 378.

60 Ms. A, p. 139.

61 Ms. A, p. 121.

62 GC, p. 304.

63 Ms. A, p. 122.

64 GC, p. 383, n. 2.

65 Pauline to Isidore Guérin, LD, Dec. 10, 1887, GC, p. 384.

66 Thérèse to Bishop Hugonin, LT 38 C, Dec. 16, 1887, GC, p. 387.

67 Testimony of Agnes of Jesus, TE, p. 29 and GC n. 389. (F from Sister Marie of the Sacred Heart according to the notebook of Sister Marie of the Incarnation, p. 114.)

68 Ms. A, p. 143
69 Testimony of François Thérèse Martin, TE, p. 177
70 Ms. A, p. 143.
71 l'Abbé Révérony to Thérèse, LC 72,

Jan. 12, 1888, GC, p. 391
72 Canon Delatroëtte to Thérèse, LC 74, Jan. 30, 1888, GC, p. 393.
73 Thérèse to Marie, LT 42, Feb. 21, 1888, GC, p. 396.

CHAPTER 4 — Carmel

1 "The Elijah Cycle," in 1 Kings, The Jerusalem Bible (New York, 1968) pp. 385-386.
2 *The Rule of St. Albert*, Hugh Clarke, O.Carm., and Bede Edwards, O.D.C., General Editors (Aylesford and Kensington, 1973), p. 79. Pope Innocent IV's amendments of 1247 are also included.
3 Ibid., no. 15, p. 87.
4 Ibid., no. 3, p. 79.
5 Ibid., no. 5, p. 81.
6 Ibid., no. 13, p. 87.
7 Ibid., nos. 10 and 14, pp. 85, 87
8 Ibid., no. 15, p. 89.
9 Ibid., no. 17, p. 91.
10 Written history of Carmelite Order, on display in Basilica of St. Thérèse, Lisieux, France.
11 The first women Carmelites date from the 15th century. Ibid.
12 Carmel de Lisieux, *Le Centenaire de la Fondation du Carmel de Lisieux*, 1838-1938, p. 8.
13 GC, p. 415.
14 See n. 64, Chapter II.
15 Ms. A, p. 247.
16 GC, p. 505, n. 1.
17 TE, p. 201.
18 TE, p. 216.
19 GC, p. 417, n. 4.
20 Except for the few nuns who dealt with the outside world.
21 The schedule summarized in the next two pages is based on DE, pp. 825-828.
22 Interview with Carmelite representative in Lisieux, July 22, 1983.
23 GC, p. 481, n. 5.
24 Piat, p. 79 (quoted from *Le Trésor du Carmel*).
25 LA, p. 180, n.

26 Interview with prioress of Lisieux Carmel, July 22, 1983.
27 DE, p. 861.
28 SU, p. 165.
29 SU, p. 166.
30 SU, p. 167.
31 SU, p. 167.
32 SU, p. 172.
33 The loan was 20,000 francs, and was never fully repaid. SU, p. 171.
34 SU, p. 172.
35 Ibid.
36 A Combes, quoted in Six, *Theèse au Carmel*, p. 193.
37 ME, p. 153.
38 SU, p. 165. The character of Mother Marie de Gonzague is a matter of controversy. In 1915 Pauline Martin and five other nuns testified to the jealous and whimsical nature of the former prioress, citing specific abuses of office. Yet Mother Gonzague was a powerful and magnetic personality, and reelected prioress for a total of 21 years. As few of the women in the convent did, she recognized the depth and potential of Thérèse Martin. For revisionist appraisals of Mother Gonzague's role vis-à-vis Thérèse see Gaucher, *La Passion de Thérèse de Lisieux*, pp. 217-220, and Laurentin, pp. 98-112.
39 IC, Book I, Ch. IX, p. 9.
40 Ms. A, p. 147.
41 Ms. A, p. 148.
42 According to Serrou and Vals, *Le Carmel, Carmélites et Carmes*, p. 44, the prioress, veiled, customarily waited inside the cloister door.
43 Ms. A, p. 148, n. 165.

44 Ms. A, p. 148.
45 GC, p. 408, n. 1 (Quoted from Mother Agnes of Jesus, Apostolic Process, pp. 370-71).
46 For descriptions of the cell see DE, p. 821, GC, p. 414 and 417, n. 2. A fascimile of Thérèse's cell is on display in the Basilica of Lisieux. In a film made in the Carmel in 1961 the actual cell is shown.
47 Ms. A, p. 148.
48 Ms. C, p. 237.
49 Ibid.
50 GC, p. 423, n. 1.
51 Ms. A, p. 150, n. 170. (Quoted from Histoire d'une Ame).
52 Ibid. These two incidents do not appear in the authenticated manuscripts of Thérèse. They apparently were added by Pauline, who resented Mother Gonzague's treatment of Thérèse.
53 Testimony of Teresa of Saint Augustine, TE, p. 195.
54 GC, p. 481, n. 5, and Letter from Mother Gonzague to Thérèse, LC 53, Sept, 1887, GC, p. 286.
55 Testimony of Marie of the Trinity, TE, p. 246-7.
56 TE, p. 201.
57 Testimony of Marie of the Trinity, TE, p. 247.
58 Testimony of Marie of the Sacred Heart, TE p. 98, and TE p. 216.
59 LA, No. 3, Sept. 2, p. 180.
60 Ms. A, p. 149.
61 Turnstyle described in interivew with Prioress of Carmel of Lisieux, July 22, 1983.
62 Letter from Thérèse to Louis Martin, LT 52, May-June 1888 (date approximated), GC, p. 434.
63 Letter from Thérèse to Louis Martin, LT 48, May 8, 1888, GC, p. 424.
64 Letter from Thérèse to Louis Martin, April 29, 1888, LT 46, GC, p. 421.
65 GC, p. 430, n. 4 (Quoted from letter from Mother Gonzague to Madame Guérin May 17, 1888.
66 Testimony of Jeanne Guérin, TE, p. 268.
67 ME, p. 172.

68 Testimony of Geneviève of Saint Teresa (Céline), TE, p. 119.
69 Ms. A, p. 151.
70 Ms. A, p. 150.
71 GC, p. 659, n. 5 (Quoted from P. Lemmonier, The Bishop's Process, 1910, 1911, p. 522).
72 GC, p. 659, n. 5 (Quoted from Circular of Sr. Teresa of Augustine, p. 5).
73 GC, p. 659, n. 5 (quoted from Preparatory Notes for the Apostolic Process, Prudence, Directors).
74 Ms. A., p. 151.
75 See P. Pichon to Thérèse, LC 82, June 18, 1888, GC, p. 436.
76 Thérèse to Father Pichon, LT 28, Oct. 23, 1887 (date approximate), GC, pp. 297-298.
77 Ms. A, p. 149.
78 Ibid.
79 LA, no. 4, p. 73.
80 Ms. A, p. 149.
81 Ms. A, p. 149 and 151. See n. 173 on p. 151.
82 GC, p. 435, n. 3 (Quoted from Sister Geneviève, Manuscript Notebooks of Sister Geneviève, IV, pp. 183-184).
83 Laurentin, p. 209. (Documented from CGE, p. 407).
84 GC, p. 437, and n. 4, p. 439. See also Ms. A, p. 154, n. 183, and LD Madame Guérin to Marie, Pauline and Thérèse, June 26, 1888, GC, p. 438.
85 Céline to Thérèse, LC 86, July 22, 1888, GC, pp. 446-7.
86 Letter from Thérèse to Céline, LT 57, July 23, 1888, GC, p. 450, and p. 451, n. 10.
87 Letter from Céline to Thérèse, LC 86, July 22, 1888, GC, pp. 446-447.
88 Letter from Thérèse to Céline, LT 57, July 23, 1888, GC, pp. 449-450.
89 Letter from Thérèse to Louis Martin, LT 58, July 31, 1888, GC, p. 451.
90 Letter from Thérèse to Louis Martin, LT 63, Sept. 30, 1888, GC, p. 461.
91 Letter from Thérèse to Céline, LT 65, October 20, 1888, GC, p. 468.
92 GC, p. 460.

93 GC, 420 and 476.
94 GC, 474. (Quoted from letter of Céline to her sisters from Honfleur, Oct. 31, 1888).
95 Mother Gonzague to Thérèse, LC 93, Dec. 6-10, 1888 (date approximate), GC, pp. 483-484.
96 Letter from Thérèse to Louis Martin, LT 72, Dec. 30, 1888, GC, p. 493.
97 GC, p. 498.
98 Letter from Thérèse to Pauline, LT 74, Jan. 6, 1889, pp. 499, 500.
99 GC, p. 505, n. 3.
100 Letter from Thérèse to Pauline, LT 76, Jan. 7, 1889, GC, p. 504.
101 Letter from Thérèse to Pauline, LT 76, Jan. 7, 1889, GC, p. 503. See GC, p. 505, n. 1.
102 Thérèse to Pauline, LT 78, Jan. 8, 1889, GC, p. 511.
103 Thérèse to Louis Martin, LT 77, Jan. 8, 1889, GC, p. 509.
104 Ms. A, pp. 154-5.
105 GC, p. 513, n. 2. (quoted from a letter from Pauline to Jeanne Guérin LaNéele, Jan., 1914).
106 Based on description in Robert Serrou et Pierre Vals, Le Carmel, Carmélites et Carmes (Paris 1957), Chap. I. According to GC 516 the custom was to cut the hair a few months later. Pauline describes the cutting of Thérèse's hair in GC 516, n. 2 (quoted from the Apostolic Process, Temperence, p. 1).
107 Ms. A, p. 155.
108 Ibid.
109 Letter from Céline to Pauline Romet, LD, Feb. 18, 1889, GC, p. 533.
110 Ibid., p. 534.
111 GC, pp. 534-5, n. 6 (quoted from a fragment of a letter from Céline to her sisters, Feb. 12, 1889, Manuscript Notebooks of Sister Geneviève, IV, p. 163).
112 GC, p. 527, and pp. 534-5, n. 6.
113 GC, p. 535, n. 6 (quoted from Sister Marie of the Incarnation's notebook, p. 229).

114 Letter from Céline to Pauline Romet, LD, Feb. 18, 1889, GC, pp. 533-534.
115 Ms. A, pp. 156-157
116 Céline to Marie, Pauline, Thérèse, LD March 1, 1889, GC, p. 538.
117 For a thorough discussion of Louis Martin's illness see Laurentin, pp. 82-92.
118 GC, p. 530, n. 4 (quoted from Sister Agnes of Jesus, Souvenirs intimes, 1905, p. 84).
119 Letter from Céline to Thérèse, LC 110, Mar. 13, 1889, GC. p. 549.
120 Letter from Thérèse to Céline, LT 86, Mar. 15, 1889, GC. p. 552.
121 Letter from Thérèse to Céline, LT 89, April 26, 1889, GC, pp. 557-558.
122 Testimony of Aimée of Jesus, TE, p. 279.
123 GC, p. 528.
124 LA, July 13, no. 18, pp. 95-96.
125 ME, p. 186.
126 LA, to Pauline, Aug. p. 258.
127 Letter from Marie Guérin to Thérèse, LC 113, May 29, 1889, GC, pp. 565-566.
128 Letter from Thérèse to Marie Guérin, LT 92, May 30, 1889, GC. pp. 567-568.
129 Ms. C, p. 249.
130 Ms. A, p. 159.
131 Ms. C, pp. 247-249.
132 Ibid.
133 See GC, p. 532, n. 5.
134 Letter from Thérèse to Marie, LT 91, End of May, 1889 (date approximate), GC, p. 564.
135 GC, p. 565, n. 4 (quoted from Manuscript Notebooks of Sister Geneviève, III, p. 103.
136 GC, p. 593.
137 Laurentin, p. 210.
138 GC, p, 520, n. 2; DE, p. 516; p. 466, n. 5.
139 Thérèse to Sister Martha of Jesus, LT 80, Jan. 10, 1889, GC p. 520.
140 GC, p. 571, (quoted from Apostolic Process 1915-16, p. 1273).
141 Eg. see Thérèse to Pauline. LT 95, July-Aug. 1889 (date approximate) GC, p. 580; Thérèse to Pauline, LT 103, May 4, 1890 (date approximate)

GC, p. 612 Thérèse to Pauline, LT
106, May 10, 1890, GC, p. 620.
142 Thérèse to Pauline, LT 103, May 4,

142 Thérèse to Pauline, LT 103, May 4,
1890 (date approximate) GC, p. 612.
143 Thérèse to Céline, LT 108, July 18,
1890, GC p. 631.

CHAPTER 5 — The Elevator

1 Thérèse to Marie, LT 111, Aug. 30-31,
1890, GC, p. 655.
2 Thérèse to Pauline, LT 112, Sept. 1,
1890, GC, p. 658.
3 Thérèse to Pauline, LT 114, Sept. 3,
1890, GC, p. 663.
4 Thérèse to Pauline, LT 115, Sept. 4,
1890, GC, p. 667.
5 Ms. A. p. 166.
6 Ibid.
7 GC, p. 645 (Quoted from *Souvenirs
intimes*, 1905, p. 88).
8 Interview with the prioress of the
Carmel of Lisieux, July 22, 1983.
9 *Story of a Soul*, p. 275.
10 Ibid.
11 Mother Gonzague to the Prioress of
the Tours Carmel, LD, Sept. 9, 1890,
GC, p. 678.
12 Sister Costard to Céline, GC, p. 607,
ft. 1, (Quoted from Manuscript
Notebooks of Sister Geneviève, IV,
pp. 204, 205).
13 Ms. A, p. 160, GC, p. 683.
14 Ibid.
15 GC, 685, n. 4 (Quoted from Preparatory Notes for the Apostolic
Process, Fortitude, proofs that she
was not spoiled, p. 3).
16 Quoted in Peter-Thomas Rohrback,
O.C.D., trans., *Photo Album of
St. Thérèse of Lisieux*, pp. 22, 23.
17 Ibid.
18 DN, 14.
19 AMC, p. 459.
20 DN, 98.
21 AMC, p. 406.
22 DN, p. 4.
23 DN, 84.
24 Thérèse to Céline, LT 108, July 18,
1890, GC, p. 632.
25 According to Sister Marie of the
Trinity, the retreat would

have been in the summer of 1890.
See GC,p. 623, n. 8 (quoted from
Mother Agnes of Jesus, Preparatory notes from the Apostolic
Process, Hope, p. 2).
26 1 Cor. 14:33.
27 Ms. A, pp. 169, 170.
28 Ms. A, p. 173.
29 Ms. A, p. 174.
30 Testimony of Sister Marie of the
Angels, TE, p. 212, and Piat, pp.
124-125
31 Gaucher, *Histoire d'Une Vie*, p.
126.
32 Ms. A, p. 34.
33 Ms. A, p. 171.
34 Ibid.
35 Testimony of Marie of the Sacred
Heart, TE, p. 101.
36 Laurentin, p. 211.
37 Testimony of Mary Magdalene of the
Blessed Sacrament, TE, p. 260.
38 Testimony of Mary Magdalene of the
Blessed Sacrament, TE, p. 264.
39 Testimony of Mary Magdalene of the
Blessed Sacrament, TE, pp 263,4.
40 According to Jean-François Six,
Thérèse de Lisieux au Carmel
(Paris 1973), p. 22, in interruption in
Mother Gonzague's tenure of office
was required by the order's consitu-
tion.
41 ME, p. 14, n. 8.
42 Testimony of Agnes of Jesus, TE, p.
31.
43 S.J. Piat, O.F.M. *Sainte Thérèse
de Lisieux à la decouverte de la
voie d'enfance*, Paris, 1964, p. 171.
44 Testimony of Martha of Jesus, TE,
p. 220.
45 Testimony of Mary Magdalene of the
Blessed Sacrament, TE, p. 262.

46 Testimony of Martha of Jesus, TE, p. 219.
47 Mother Gonzague to the Visitation Convent, DE, p. 137, n. 49.
48 DE, p. 30, and Gaucher, *La Passion de Thérèse de Lisieux*, pp. 40-41.
49 ME, pp. 100-101.
50 ME, pp. 186-187, and ME, p. 24.
51 Ms. C, p. 207.
52 According to De Meester, though the monastery had two copies of the Bible, young nuns were not authorized to read the complete Bible, p. 77.
53 Ms. C, pp. 207, 208. Though Thérèse wrote this explanation of her discovery of the scriptural basis for her "little way" in 1897, it is very likely to have occurred in late 1894 or early 1895. See Meester, pp. 81-84.
54 ME, p. 124.
55 ME, p. 125.
56 ME, p. 126.
57 ME, p. 129.
58 Testimony of Geneviève of St. Teresa, TE, p. 132.
59 TE, p. 217.
60 Testimony of Agnes of Jesus, TE, p. 33; Testimony of Marie of the Sacred Heart, TE, p. 83.

61 Laurentin, pp. 211, 212.
62 Ms. A, p. 14.
63 Ms. A, p. 29.
64 Ms. A, p. 170.
65 Piat, p. 79.
66 Gaucher, *Histoire d' Une Vie*, p. 157.
67 Ms. A, pp 180-181.
68 Testimony of Geneviève of Saint Teresa, TE, p. 128; Ms. A, p. 180.
69 ME, p. 89.
70 Clarke, *Story of a Soul*, pp. 276-287. Father Le Monnier, who examined Thérèse's offering, made only one change, substituting the words "immense desires" for "infinite desires." Ibid, p. 46. Testimony of Agnes of Jesus, TE, pp. 46.
71 Testimony of Agnes of Jesus, TE, pp. 46.
72 ME, p. 90.
73 ME, pp. 91, 92.
74 Testimony of Agnes of Jesus, TE, p. 33.
75 Laurentin, p. 213; Gaucher, *Histoire d'Une Vie*, pp. 163-164.
76 Quoted in Six, *Thérèse de Lisieux au Carmel*, pp. 231-232.
77 CL, p. 269.
78 Gaucher, *Histoire d'Une Vie*, p. 165.

CHAPTER 6 — The Dark Night

1 Ms. C, pp. 210-211. Thérèse used the pronoun "our" in referring to her lamp, since technically she owned nothing.
2 Ibid.
3 Testimony of Marie of the Sacred Heart, TE, p. 98.
4 Self-flagellation.
5 Testimony of Marie of the Trinity, TE, p. 243.
6 Ms. C, p. 211.
7 Ibid.
8 Ibid.
9 Ibid.
10 Ms. C, pp. 211-213.
11 DE, p. 801.

12 Robert Koch, "The Aetiology of Tuberculosis," in Logan Clendening, M.D., editor, *The Source Book of Medical History* (New York, 1960), pp. 392-406.
13 X-Rays were discovered in 1895, and first used as a diagnostic tool for TB in 1896.
14 René Laënnec, "Mediate Ascultation," in Clendening, pp. 315-328.
15 Koch, "The Aetiology of Tuberculosis," in Clendening, p. 393.
16 Fred A. Mettler, ed., *History of Medicine*, p. 471.
17 GC, p. 629, n. 3
18 Gaucher, *Histoire d'Une Vie*, p.

p. 170 (quoted from CG, 1188), and DE 807.

19 DE, p. 857

20 Quoted in LA, p. 21, and DE, p. 30 (LT 192, July 7, 1896).

21 Thérèse was assigned to the linen room after the 1896 elections. LA, p. 95. July 13, No. 18. Also see ME, p. 213.

22 Introduction to *Story of a Soul*, p. XIII.

23 Ms B, pp. 192-195.

24 Marie to Thérèse, September 16, 1896, CL, pp. 287, 288.

25 Thérèse to Marie, September 17, 1896, CL, p. 288.

26 Testimony of Teresa of St. Augustine, TE, p. 195.

27 Testimony of Marie of the Trinity, TE, p. 243.

28 Ms. C, pp. 217, 218.

29 DE, p. 31.

30 ME, p. 73.

31 DE, p. 828.

32 Testimony of Agnes of Jesus, TE, p. 66.

33 DE, pp. 32 and 148.

34 July 13, No. 18, LA, p. 96.

35 Ms. A, pp. 13 and 15.

36 LA, p. 18 (quoted from DE, p. 35).

37 LA, pp. 22, 23, n. 31 and 24.

38 May 18, No. 1, LA, p. 45.

39 May 20, No. 1, LA, p. 46.

40 May 21-26, No. 3, LA, p. 47.

41 DE, p. 150-151.

42 DE, p. 152.

43 ME, p. 214.

44 May 30, No. 1, LA, p. 53.

45 Testimony of Agnes of Jesus, TE, p. 34.

46 LA, p. 23.

47 Marie Guérin to Isidore Guérin, June 5, 1897, LA, p. 271.

48 LA, p. 54.

49 Marie Guérin to Isidore Guérin, June 5, 1897, LA, p. 271.

50 Ms. C, p. 214.

51 Ms. C, p. 219.

52 Ibid.

53 Ms. C, p. 220.

54 Ibid.

55 Ibid.

56 Ms. C, p. 221.

57 Ms. C, p. 222.

58 Ms. C, p. 223.

59 Ms. C, p. 227.

60 Ms. C, p. 228.

61 Ms. C, p. 234.

62 Ms. C, p. 242.

63 Ms. C, pp. 242, 243.

64 Ms. C, p. 253.

65 Ms. C, p. 254.

66 Ms. C, pp. 254, 256.

67 Ms. C, p. 258, n. 352.

68 Ms. C, pp. 258 9.

69 LA, p. 71.

70 July 3, No. 1, LA, p. 71.

71 July 7, No. 4 and 5, pp. 77, 78.

72 DE, p. 160.

73 July 8, No. 1, LA, p. 79, and Letter from Marie Guérin to Isidore Guérin, July 12, 1897, LC, pp. 276, 7.

CHAPTER 7 — Last Days

1 Sister Marie-Antoinette died of tuberculosis November 4, 1896, Gaucher, *Histoire d'Une Vie*, n. 77, pp. 214, 215.

2 Marie Guérin to Isidore Guérin, July 8, 1897, LA, pp. 272, 3.

3 July 7, No. 5, LA, p. 78.

4 DE, p. 805. The bacillus may have been present much earlier. When Thérèse was not quite four years old, Zélie had written of a strange whistle in her chest. See Zélie to Madame Guérin, Nov. 12, 1876, CF, p. 323. In this context, Jean-François Six in his psychological study published in 1973, *Thérèse de Lisieux au Carmel*, cites medical research published in the 1960s indicating a correlation between the activation of the TB bacillus in young people (specifically pulmonary TB), and certain psychological disturbances such as depression or a rupture in the victim's home life, pp. 314-319

5 Gaucher, *La Passion de Thérèse de Lisieux*, pp. 218-219.

6 See René and Jean Dubos, *The White Plague, Tuberculosis, Man and Society* (Boston, 1952), and Six, *Thérèse de Lisieux au Carmel*, pp. 312-313.

7 In her letters of July 20 and 22, Marie Guérin alludes to more lung damage, the formation of cavities, and to Dr. de Cornière stating that "the sickness pursues its course." This phrase suggests that by this time Marie Guérin understands from the doctor that Thérèse is suffering from TB. See Marie Guérin to Isidore Guérin, July 20, 1897, LA, p. 281, and Marie Guérin to Madame Guérin, July 22, 1897, LA, p. 282.

8 Ms. A, p. 181.

9 July 7, No. 3, LA, p. 77 (quoted from Job 13:15)

10 Laurentin, p. 139.

11 July 7, No. 2, LA, p. 77.

12 July 17, LA, p. 102.

13 August 3, No. 1. LA, p. 129.

14 July 16, LA, p. 100

15 DE, p. 164.

16 July 20, No. 4, LA, p. 104.

17 Ibid.

18 July 25, No. 2, LA, p. 109.

19 July 27, No. 9, LA, p. 114.

20 Marie Guérin to Isidore Guérin, July 10, 1897, LA, p. 275.

21 LA, p. 298.

22 July 13, No. 6, LA, p. 92.

23 From Marie Guérin to Isidore Guérin, July 8, 1897, LA, p. 275.

24 Ibid., p. 274.

25 August 7, No. 5, LA, p. 141.

26 Aug. 9, No. 3, LA, p. 143.

27 July 30, No. 2, LA, p. 118; August 23, No. 7, LA, p. 165.

28 Marie Guérin to Madame Guérin, July 30, 1897, LA, p. 283.

29 Marie Guérin to Isidore Guérin, July 31, 1897, LA, pp. 283, 284.

30 July 31, No. 3, LA, p. 122.

31 July 29, No. 2, LA, pp. 115-116 and Gaucher, *La Passion de Thérèse de Lisieux*, p. 99.

32 August 1, No. 2, p. 126.

33 August 4, No. 7, LA, p. 132.

34 DE, p. 168.

35 Marie Guérin to Isidore Guérin, August 5, 1897, LA, p. 286.

36 August 5, No. 4, p. 134.

37 August 6, footnote, LA, p. 138, and DE, p. 520.

38 DE, 168-169, and Gaucher, *La Passion de Thérèse de Lisieux*, p. 83.

39 DE, 170.

40 LA, p. 295, and Dr. Francis La Néele to Isidore Guérin, August 26, 1897, LA, p. 289.

41 Marie Guérin to Madame Guérin, August 17, 1897, LA, p. 286.

42 Dr. Francis La Néele to Isidore Guérin, August 26, 1897, LA, pp. 289, 290.

43 Marie Guérin to Madame Guérin, August 22, 1897, LA, pp. 287, 288.

44 LA, pp. 162, 163 footnote (quoted from Mother Agnes's green copybooks).

45 Testimony of Marie of the Sacred Heart, TE, p. 92.

46 LA, p. 203, footnote (cited from Mother Agnes' green copybooks)

47 LA, p. 172, footnote (quoted from Mother Agnes' green copybooks).

48 DE, p. 175.

49 August 28, No. 2, LA, p. 173.

50 DE, p. 175.

51 August 28, No. 3, LA, p. 173.

52 DE, p. 177.

53 Ibid.

54 DE, p. 177.

55 Gaucher, *La Passion de Thérèse de Lisieux*, p. 105.

56 LA, pp. 176 and 184; DE, p. 178.

57 August 31, No. 5, p. 176.

58 Céline to Madame Guérin, Beginning of September, 1897, LA, p. 291.

59 LA, p. 157, footnote (cited from Sister Agnes' green copybooks).

60 June 5, No. 4, DE, p. 221.

61 August 20, No. 13, p. 159.

62 August 21, No. 3, p. 161.

63 LA, p. 257.

64 August 7, No. 4, LA, p. 140.

65 Thérèse to Céline, LT 89, April 26, 1889, GC, pp. 557, 558.

66 July 10, No. 1, LA, p. 84.

67 DE, p. 180.
68 September 13, No. 1, LA, p. 189.
69 LA, pp. 258, 259.
70 To Marie, September 17, 1897, pp. 242, 243.
71 September 24, No. 10, LA, p. 199.
72 September 24, No. 3, LA, p. 198.
73 Madame Guérin to Jeanne La Néele, September 25, 1897, LA, p. 291.
74 September 29, No. 1, LA, p. 201.
75 September 29, No. 5, LA, p. 202.
76 LA, p. 203, footnote (cited from Sister Agnes' green copybook).

77 September 30, LA, p. 204.
78 DE, p. 145, n. 103.
79 DE, 555.
80 September 30, LA, pp. 205, 206.
81 Testimony of Sister Marie of the Trinity, TE, p. 255.
82 September 30, LA, p. 206.
83 DE, p. 186.
84 September 30, LA, pp. 206, 207.
85 Testimony of Sister Mary Magdalene, TE, p. 264.
86 Testimony of Françoise-Thérèse Martin, TE, p. 180.

CHAPTER 8 — Epilogue

1 DE, 821
2 DE, 15.5.4, b), p. 419.
3 Testimony of Martha of Jesus, TE, p. 226.
4 Story of a Soul, Introduction, p. xv.
5 Beevers, p. 127.
6 TE, p. 272.
7 Ibid., p. 273.
8 Testimony of Godefroy Madelaine, O. Praem., TE, pp. 273, 274.
9 Beevers, pp. 127, 128.
10 Testimony of Agnes of Jesus, TE, p. 71.
11 Ibid.
12 Testimony of Godefroy Madelaine, O. Praem., TE, p. 274.
13 Quotes taken from Sainte Thérèse de l'Enfant-Jesus, manuscrits autobiographiques (Lisieux 1957), pp. 181, 109, 84, and Sainte Thérèse de l'Enfant-Jesus, Histoire d'Une Ame, (Lisieux 1949), pp. 111, 118, 77, 66.
14 Testimony of Thomas Nimmo Taylor, TE, pp. 74, 75, and Gaucher Histoire d'Une Vie, p. 225.
15 Gaucher, Histoire d'Une Vie, p. 225.
16 Gaucher, Histoire d'Une Vie, p. 224.
17 Testimony of Agnes of Jesus, TE, p. 70.
18 Ibid.
19 TE, p. 7. This was not Bishop Hugonin, who died in 1898. Isidore Guérin died in 1909.

20 CL, p. 378.
21 Testimony of Agnes of Jesus, TE, p. 71.
22 TE, p. 7.
23 Testimony of Aimée of Jesus, TE, p. 279.
24 LA, pp. 302, 303.
25 Testimony of Martha of Jesus, TE, p. 228.
26 Testimony of Marie of the Trinity, TE, p. 255.
27 Testimony of Agnes of Jesus, TE, p. 71.
28 Testimony of Geneviève of Saint Teresa, TE, pp. 162, 163.
29 ME, pp. 224, 225.
30 Father François de Sainte-Marie, the editor of manuscrits autobiographiques, discusses the question in his commentary in Rohrback, Photo Album of St. Thérèse of Lisieux.
31 Ibid, p. 26.
32 Ibid.
33 Ibid. p. 46
34 Ibid.
35 Laurentin, p. 217.
36 Ibid., p. 218.
37 Shower of Roses, No. 21, p. 31.
38 Cases are all taken from the 1912 edition of The Shower of Roses, published by the Carmel of Lisieux.
39 Quoted in V. Sackville-West, The Eagle and the Dove, p. 175.

40 "Décret d'Approbation des Miracles pour la Canonisation," March 19, 1925, quoted in *Pluie de Roses* (Archives of the Carmel of Lisieux), p. 614.

41 *Pluie de Roses*, p. 153.

42 Ibid.

43 *The New York Times*, May 18, 1925, p. 2.

44 Ibid., p. 1.

45 All details of the canonization were taken from *The New York Times*, May 18, 1925, pp. 1, 2.

46 Laurentin, p. 36.

47 Ibid., p. 37

48 LA, July 8, No. 16, p. 82

INDEX

171

Laënnec, René, 110-112
La Néele, Dr. Francis, 89, 111, 128,
    134-135, 136-137, 150
Laurentin, René, 129
Leo XIII, Pope, 40-42, 46, 143
Lepelletier, Father, 31, 43-44
Les Buissonnets, 2, 14, 28, 75-76
Lisieux, France, 2 et passim
    in 1870s, 15
    Martins move to, 14
    today, 2
Louise of St. Germain, Sister, 152

Madelaine, Father Godefroy, 144-145
Marie-Ange of the Child Jesus, Mother,
    147
Marie de Gonzague, Mother (Marie-
    Adèle-Rosalie-Davy de Vir-
    ville), 32 et passim
    death, 148
    description and temperament, 32,
        56-57, 162n
    early meeting and correspondence
        with Thérèse, 32-33
    and Manuscript C, 119-120
    opinion and treatment of Thérèse, 59,
        60-61, 63, 67, 89
    as prioress, 57-58, 106, 165n
    publication of Thérèse's writings,
        144-145
    and Thérèse's entrance to Carmel,
        41, 47
    and Thérèse's last illness and death,
        111, 115-116, 134, 135-136, 141, 142
Marie of the Angels, Sister, 54, 61, 64,
    79
Marie of the Trinity, Sister, 104,
    107-108, 115, 142, 148
Martha of Jesus, Sister, 54, 62, 76, 88,
    99, 100, 148
Martin, Céline (Sister Geneviève of St.
    Thérèse), 9 et passim
    death, 155
    and illness of Louis Martin, 65-67,
        70-71
    and image of Thérèse in art, 148-151
    and offering as victim to Divine
        Love, 102
    profession, 105
    romanticism of, 31, 40, 72, 89
    as Thérèse's confidante (1887), 31
    and Thérèse's final illness, 131, 134,
        135, 137, 141
172

trip to Rome, 39, 41, 44
Martin, Hélène, 9
Martin, Léonie, 9 et passim
    and the convent, 27-28, 33, 48
    buys Thérèse's habit, 144
    death, 155
    during Thérèse's final illness, 117,
        136
    and Thérèse's childhood illness, 21
Martin, Louis (father), 2 et passim
    background and personality, 12
    death, 89
    at Thérèse's taking of habit, 69-70
    illness, 33, 65-67, 70-71
    last visit to Carmel, 86
    moves to Lisieux, 13-15
    and Thérèse, 2-3, 15, 33, 37-39, 44-45,
        48, 62-63, 66-68, 86
    and Zélie, 12-13
Martin, Marie (Sister Marie of the Sa-
    cred Heart), 13 et passim
    death, 155
    during Thérèse's final illness and
        death, 133, 141
    enters Carmel, 26-27
    and Manuscript B, 112-115
    offering as Victim to God's Love, 104
    stills Thérèse's teenage scruples, 25
    and Thérèse's childhood illness, 20-22
    and Thérèse's First Communion,
        22-23
Martin, Pauline (Mother Agnes of
    Jesus), 11 et passim
    death, 155
    describes Thérèse's death, 141-142
    describes Thérèse's temptation to
        suicide, 135-136
    edits Thérèse's writing, 144, 145-146
    elected prioress, 87
    enters Carmel, 18-19
    influence on young Thérèse, 16, 18,
        23-24
    last conversations with Thérèse,
        117-119, 126-127, 129-142
    letters from Zélie, 11, 13
    and Manuscript A, 100-101, 104, 117,
        119
    relationship with Thérèse in Carmel,
        64, 68, 73, 100, 102, 104, 117,
        126-127, 129-143
    and Thérèse's entrance to Carmel,
        18, 23-24, 32, 36, 43-44, 47-48
    and Thérèse's illness in childhood, 21